·*microwave*·
VEGETABLE
COOKING

Tomatoes stuffed with spaghetti squash (see p. 112); Spinach parcels with liver pâté (see p. 116).

·*microwave*·
VEGETABLE
COOKING

Original Vegetable Dishes for All Occasions

JUDY JACKSON

MACDONALD ORBIS

For my mother, Tess Blackburn

A Macdonald Orbis Book

© Macdonald & Co (Publishers) Ltd 1989
Text © Judy Jackson 1989

First published in Great Britain in 1989
by Macdonald & Co (Publishers) Ltd
London & Sydney

A member of Maxwell Pergamon Publishing Corporation plc

British Library Cataloguing in Publication Data
Jackson, Judy
Microwave vegetable cooking.
1. Food. Vegetable dishes prepared using microwave ovens–
–Recipes
I. Title
641.6'5

ISBN 0–356–17568–5

Typeset by Bookworm Typesetting, Manchester
Printed and bound in Spain by
Imprenta Hispano-Americana S. A

Senior Editor: Joanna Lorenz
Text Editor: Felicity Jackson
Senior Art Editor: Clive Hayball
Designer: Chris Branfield
Photographer: Alan Newnham
Assisted by Ken Field
Stylist: Sue Russell
Home Economist: Dolly Meers
Illustrations: Annie Ellis

Macdonald & Co (Publishers) Ltd
Headway House
66-73 Shoe Lane
London EC4P 4AB

ACKNOWLEDGEMENTS
I should like to thank my husband Michael and my four
sons for their help while I was writing the book. I must also
mention Jacques Loussier, who, unknowingly, has given
me hours of pleasure with his recordings of Bach which I
played throughout the recipe testing! Finally, I am grateful
to the Panasonic Test Kitchen at Slough, Berks, for the loan
of a Dimension 4 Combination oven.

CONTENTS

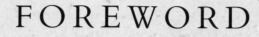

FOREWORD

From the moment a child throws his first spoonful of spinach across the room he is demonstrating a fairly traditional view of vegetables! For years they have been overcooked, maltreated and misunderstood. A cookery expert called Mrs Roundell offered this advice a hundred years ago: 'Plenty of water is especially necessary in boiling all sorts of cabbage, including Brussels sprouts, for it reduces the smell. Even if a little water boils over, there is sure to be a nauseous smell all over the house.'

In the 1960's, while the French were serving vegetables as a respectable course on their own, English restaurants were offering side plates piled with unlikely mixtures of cauliflower cheese, garlicky ratatouille and heavily buttered spinach. Anything unusual was a complete mystery to the general public. I once asked for an aubergine in a small, suburban shop. The puzzled assistant disappeared into the back and emerged carrying an avocado. 'I knew we had some', he said, 'but they're rather hard and green'.

With the arrival of nouvelle cuisine, things started to change. Chefs dictated that portions had to be tiny and beans should be crisp. But if you loved vegetables you were still likely to be frustrated. When the main course arrived there would be five small slices of rare lamb in the middle of the plate, surrounded by an artistic arrangement of three minute potato balls and a couple of mange-tout.

Today the scene is quite different. Our eyes have been opened to the wonderful range of vegetables in the world. Boxes of colourful produce are flown to this country from Cyprus, Israel, California and Chile, and we are no longer restricted to our own seasonal harvests.

But the greatest change of all has been in the cooking. In the early days of microwaving, speed and convenience were all that mattered. Taste and appearance were often sacrificed in the interests of producing quick and easy meals. But with vegetables there is no compromise. The moist heat combined with fast cooking in very little liquid produces results that are incomparable. Microwaved vegetables are actually *better*. Saucepans and steamers evaporate the flavour and dull the colours. With the new microwave method, a vegetable that is cooked can be brilliant to look at and a delight to eat.

It has taken years for most of us to appreciate what vegetarians have known for some time: that vegetables are not just decorative side dishes—they can be served on their own as a savoury course, bringing interest and colour to a classic meal.

Andre Simon, writing about food and wine just after the war, believed that vegetarians 'should never be asked to any civilized meal'. He would eat his words if he could see what imagination and skilful microwaving can do to vegetables today.

INTRODUCTION

—————— HOW TO USE THIS BOOK ——————

The recipes are divided into 7 chapters and include about 45 different vegetables. The early chapters give detailed instructions for preparing and cooking most of them. If you are looking for a particular vegetable you should look it up in the index where you will find suggestions for recipes. If, on the other hand, you are wondering what to serve, you would do better to look through the various courses for ideas. Much of the food is inter-changeable. For example, some of the starters, side dishes and salads would make a vegetarian main course. Similarly, almost any recipe in the book could be used to begin a meal.

—————— MICROWAVE INFORMATION ——————

Although it sounds rather obvious advice, I would strongly recommend you to study the operating instructions and any cookery book which comes with your particular cooker, as there are so many types on the market. This will give you the guidelines for the cooking techniques and various settings you will need to use.

I tested the recipes in this book with 2 cookers—one with 9 power levels and the other with 5. For most purposes I used the highest setting. For a few dishes which need gentler cooking, I refer to Low or Medium, followed by a number. This was the corresponding number on the 1–9 scale. When you are choosing the exact power level for your own cooker, it might help you to refer to the following table:

HIGH	100% power	(600–700W)
MEDIUM	60% power	(360–420W)
LOW	30% power	(180–210W)

No times are given for thawing as it is impossible to be precise. The newer cookers with 'cyclic defrost' facility might take longer, although the programmed resting periods ensure a more even result.

────────── COMBINATION COOKING ──────────

Most vegetables are best cooked in a simple microwave cooker. Some foods are better brown and crisp on top and the combination cooker achieves this without overcooking the centre. As pre-set programmes vary considerably from one model to another, I have given approximate temperatures and corresponding power levels. You can set a dish to brown without watching or burning it, but the time it takes may vary as it depends on several other factors too: whether you have a fan-assisted cooker, how deep the container is and where it is in relation to the heat source. It is always possible to achieve the same result with a preheated conventional oven or grill.

────────── SPECIAL EQUIPMENT ──────────

There is only one new piece of equipment you might need to buy, and that is a large oval microwave dish with a vented cover. You can then arrange the vegetables in a single layer with very little liquid so that the moisture is retained and the steam released. It avoids the problems of finding microwavable clingfilm.

For soups you can use a heavy (non-metal) casserole but remember that cooking food in thick containers takes longer. For example, if you melt butter on a plate it will soften quicker than in a straight-sided pot.

For stuffed dishes or those you want to brown, you will need toughened glass or china. Round dishes are best for even cooking.

Jugs, bowls and sauce boats are ideal for making small amounts of sauce. Coffee cups or ramekins (without metal rims) are good for mousselines and timbales and you never have to grease them before cooking. If you want to make a terrine in a ring, you can improvise by placing an upturned glass in the centre of a round dish. This removes the centre or 'cold spot' which always takes longer to cook, and is especially useful for quiche mixtures which cannot be stirred.

────────── OTHER TECHNIQUES AND TOOLS ──────────

There are some things you can't do in the microwave–you will need to boil water in a kettle for skinning tomatoes; making pancakes for part of a recipe should only be attempted in the usual way, and I personally think onions and aubergines are better fried in a pan over direct heat.

Some people believe that a microwave with a turntable eliminates the need to stir food and this is generally true for vegetables as there is no need to move them around during cooking. However, all sauces need to be stirred frequently and delicate dishes should be stopped periodically to check the cooking process.

Amongst your 'batterie de cuisine' you should include:

•

a good chopping board

•

an assortment of sharp and serrated knives

•

a small vegetable parer (or potato peeler) which removes the outside skins or makes wafer-thin slices

•

a sieve

You will need a blender for soups, and a food processor is useful for pâtés and dips.

QUANTITIES

Most of the recipes in this book, unless otherwise stated, are designed to serve 4. You can probably assess how filling they will be by reading the ingredients, but remember that appetites vary enormously and what one person would regard as an adequate starter, another might consider just a mouthful! In general it is usually better to make more dishes than you think you will need–especially if you are entertaining.

If you want to increase the quantities in the recipes you will have to alter the timing. Unlike a conventional oven where larger amounts still take the same time to cook, if you double the amount of vegetables in a microwave you will have to cook them for half as long again. As a rough guide, if 450 g/1 lb takes 8 minutes, 900 g/2 lb will take 12 minutes. It is often simpler to prepare double quantities and just repeat the cooking process.

NOTES FOR VEGETARIANS

The idea of the book is not to exclude meat and fish completely but to show how vegetables can be enjoyed in many different courses and not just on the side. If you are a vegetarian you can see at a glance by the titles which recipes are unsuitable for you, with the exception of the soups. Nearly all these are based on vegetable stocks but a few do depend on meat or chicken for a stronger flavour and are unsuitable for vegetarians. For some of the main course dishes there is a list of suggested substitutes in the Appendix. It is always possible to make a substantial meal from any of the recipes, either by increasing the quantities or by combining 2 or more dishes.

GENERAL ADVICE ON MICROWAVING

The first thing to remember is that the timing is usually extremely short, so 30 seconds can be crucial. When assessing how long something will take, two factors should be taken into account: your particular cooker and your own personal taste. Power outputs vary in different cookers and a 'cooked' vegetable to one person may seem almost raw to someone else (my own preference is for the vegetables to be slightly crisp).

It never does any harm to open the door to see if the food is cooked, and it is far better to do this, then carry on for an extra minute, than leave it to chance and find that it is irretrievably overdone.

The following are useful hints for cooking vegetables:

•

use very little water – the more you add the longer the
vegetables take to cook
•
arrange them in a single layer, with the tenderest parts towards the
centre, then cover with a vented lid
•
season lightly after cooking. Add a little salt and pepper,
cover the pot and shake gently to distribute the seasoning
•
preheat the serving plates. Microwaved food is of course hot,
but as the cooking containers stay cool, you must expect a
rapid loss of heat.

CHOOSING VEGETABLES

If you like vegetables, you'll already know what to look for when you go shopping. Sometimes you may think it is an economy to buy cheap items but you should always reject anything that looks wilted, damaged or old as it won't get any better once it is cooked. You should aim for the firmest and freshest produce, so it's worth looking for a greengrocer with an interesting and varied supply. You can then find out the days or times when fresh deliveries arrive.

Don't be embarrassed to ask your greengrocer to find unusual things for you, or to pick out the sizes you want. If you don't have a good local shop, go to the largest supermarket. The advantage here is that you can pick out exactly what you want from a large and colourful variety. When you go shopping, be flexible and change your plans if you see something fresh in the market that you hadn't thought about.

Whenever possible, it is better to buy produce that is in season as natural ripening improves the flavour. If it is locally grown it will also be cheaper. Food that is grown to withstand air travel can never be quite the same, so it is a good idea to avoid it except perhaps in winter when it may be the only choice.

STORING VEGETABLES

Ideally you should never store vegetables at all, and should use them as soon as possible after they have been picked. The most obvious examples are asparagus and corn on the cob, which have a totally different taste even a few hours after they have been cut. However, for most people with a busy life and no access to local farms, it is practical to think about the best way to keep vegetables fresh.

Potatoes, onions, carrots and other root vegetables should be stored in a cool, airy place. Almost everything else is better kept covered in the refrigerator. Beetroot and mushrooms should be used very quickly as they do not keep well. Spinach and watercress also have a very short life and are best used on the day they are bought.

FROZEN AND CANNED VEGETABLES

The recipes have all been designed with fresh vegetables in mind. In a very few cases the frozen product will do – for example, peas and corn, and leaf spinach (but only if it is to be chopped). The resulting taste and texture will, however, be noticeably different. It is best to avoid all canned vegetables, with the exception of tomatoes which make an excellent winter sauce.

HERBS

Dried herbs have a very strong flavour and are not recommended for the dishes in this book. Some herbs freeze well and are very good for sauces. Oregano, basil, rosemary and chives thaw quickly and their flavour is almost as good as fresh. When you need herbs in larger quantities or specially for decoration, such as dill, parsley, chervil or long chives, then only the freshest ones will do.

FLAVOURINGS

It is hard to define correct seasoning as tastes vary so much. For this reason I have given no quantities but just say 'salt' and 'pepper'–usually meaning freshly ground black pepper. If you sprinkle salt on to vegetables before they are microwaved it toughens them, so it is better to add it later or use a lightly salted stock. If you don't have time to make your own vegetable stock (see p.44) or the recipe only requires a few spoonfuls, a quick solution is to use a chicken flavour powder which contains no animal products. A level teaspoon of the powder, mixed with 450 ml/¾ pint boiling water and strained, makes a mild stock to sprinkle over vegetables or to intensify the flavour of soups.

Garlic, lemon and herbs are included in many of the recipes. Spices like pepper or coriander, and especially nutmeg, should always be freshly ground. Here again, you can alter the quantity to taste.

PREPARATION

With vegetables, it is not the cooking that takes the time but the preparation. If you have ever eaten in a Japanese restaurant you will realize that the skill is in the way the foods have been cut. They are even in size and arranged to complement each other in colour, shape and texture. This technique is exactly what is needed for microwave cookery. If the vegetables are unevenly cut they will be unevenly cooked. It is always better to have everything washed, prepared and sliced–ready to be cooked at the last moment.

Some vegetables need 'double preparation': you need to remove the hairy choke from a cooked artichoke, or the tough skin from a broad bean. Also, you should salt, drain and part-cook aubergines before frying them.

Starters

A starter doesn't have to be an elaborately
planned first course. It can be anything
you feel like eating before you get down to
the serious part of the meal. It's interesting to
know how many people head straight for the
refrigerator when they walk in, peering
inside to see what looks appetising. It could
be a bowl of radishes with some unsalted
butter, a pile of cooked French beans, some
cherry tomatoes or a couple of rice-stuffed
vine leaves. Put them into separate glass
bowls in the middle of the table and open a
bottle of chilled wine and you've already got
a starter. The great chef Boulestin had a very
sensible approach: 'When entertaining one's
friends, one should have the same sort of food
one has all the time – only more of it.'

Unlike meat or fish, vegetables are naturally
beautiful and need very little to make them look
appealing.

The starters in this chapter are designed to show you
how to microwave vegetables on their own. The basic
techniques are used throughout the book, so it might
be helpful to glance through these recipes first.

Asparagus with melted herb butter

You don't need string or steamers with microwaved asparagus. Just be as generous as you can and buy the freshest possible produce.

900 g/2 lb fresh asparagus
75 g/3 oz butter, slightly softened
3 tbsp chopped fresh herbs, such as chives, dill or parsley
3 tsp fresh lime or lemon juice
salt and black pepper

1 Trim off the tough ends of the asparagus and scrape the last few inches of the stems with a vegetable peeler. Wash them briefly and drain.
2 Arrange half the asparagus in a single layer in a rectangular dish. Sprinkle over about 4 tbsp water and cook, covered, on HIGH for about 6 minutes. Keep warm and repeat with remaining asparagus.
3 Meanwhile, mash the butter with the chopped herbs and lime or lemon juice, mixing them well. Season with salt and pepper.
4 Drain the cooked asparagus and divide it equally between 4 warmed plates.
5 Spread the softened herb butter gently over the tips and serve immediately.

Note: some people may prefer hot melted butter – which I find a bit oily – but if you do, just heat the butter on HIGH until it melts – about 1 minute.

Cold broccoli with walnut vinaigrette

A French chef at the turn of the century believed that 'for a green salad there is nothing better than oil made of crushed walnuts'. Fragrant nut oils have recently come back into fashion and they certainly enhance cooked vegetables too.

450 g/1 lb broccoli
3 tbsp vegetable stock
salt and black pepper
Walnut Vinaigrette
4 tbsp walnut oil
2 tbsp unscented oil
2 tbsp wine vinegar
¼ tsp mustard
pinch sugar

1 Trim the ends of the broccoli and cut them lengthwise so that the stalks are fairly thin and even. Rinse and drain.
2 Arrange the florets in a dish so that the stems are pointing outwards and the heads are towards the centre. Sprinkle with the stock, cover and cook on HIGH for 4 minutes. Season lightly.
3 Let stand for a few minutes while you prepare the vinaigrette then drain off any liquid.
4 Put the oils, vinegar, mustard, sugar, salt and pepper into an empty wine bottle with a cork. Shake the sauce vigorously until it is thick.
5 To serve immediately, leave the broccoli to cool slightly, then spoon on a little of the sauce. Serve the rest separately.

Note: Microwaved vegetables have a brilliant colour shortly after cooking. It is generally best to eat them straight away, but in the case of a cold dish like this, you can prepare it in advance. In that case, sprinkling with vinaigrette would make the vegetables dull and limp, so you should only do this as you bring them to the table.

Warm tomatoes with mozzarella

The colours of the Italian flag are used to make the famous antipasto salad with tomato, mozzarella and avocado. The cheese is very bland when cold, but is wonderful melted. You can serve this dish with hot French bread or even turn it into 'instant pizzas' by spooning it on to toasted muffins and adding olives, mushrooms or anchovies.

4 large tomatoes
350 g/12 oz mozzarella cheese
2 tsp tomato purée
1 tsp olive oil
salt and pepper
pinch sugar
1 tbsp chopped fresh oregano

1 Slice the tomatoes and arrange in circles on 4 small plates.
2 Cut the cheese into thin slices and divide into 4 portions.
3 Mix together the tomato purée, oil, salt, pepper and sugar and brush the mixture over the sliced tomatoes.
4 Alternate overlapping slices of the tomatoes and cheese and cook 2 at a time, as the microwave will probably not be large enough to take all 4. Preheat a separate grill to keep the first 2 warm.
5 Cook on HIGH for 2 minutes, turning the plates after 1½ minutes to make sure the cheese melts evenly.
6 Repeat with the next 2 plates, then serve immediately, sprinkled with the chopped oregano.

Globe artichokes with vinaigrette sauce

I often wonder how the first person ever discovered that the thistly artichoke was edible – and how they persevered through all those tough leaves, discarding the hairy choke and finally arriving at the sweet tender base. It's one of the most leisurely starters – never to be hurried – but that doesn't mean that preparing it has to take ages too.

4 large artichokes, weighing about 400 g/14 oz
*   each*
9 tbsp olive oil
3 tbsp wine vinegar
1 tsp French mustard
pinch sugar
salt and pepper

1 Lay the artichokes on their sides. Using a very sharp knife, cut off each stem close to the base and cut across the top of the leaves. Then with either a knife or scissors, cut across the points of the lower, outer leaves. Immediately wash the artichokes and drop them into a large quantity of acidulated water (water containing the juice and empty halves of a lemon).
2 Cook 2 artichokes at a time; rinse and dry them well and place on a small dish. Sprinkle over 4 tbsp boiling water (to which you have added a little salt). Cover and cook on HIGH for 6 minutes. Turn the artichokes over so that the base is uppermost and cook for another 4 minutes. Repeat with the other 2 artichokes.
3 Leave to cool slightly and then open out the top leaves carefully. Remove the hairy choke with a spoon, being careful not to damage the heart while you do this.
4 Put the oil, vinegar, mustard and seasonings in a screw-top jar and shake well. Keep in the jar to shake again just before serving.

Peperonata

Opinions vary about whether or not to skin peppers. All that grilling until they are charred seems a bit pointless to me, but pieces of detached tomato skin in a dish are another matter and they are easy to remove beforehand.

3 tbsp olive oil
1 onion, chopped
1 fat garlic clove, crushed
350 g/12 oz red peppers, deseeded and sliced
275 g/10 oz ripe tomatoes
½ tsp sugar
salt and pepper
1 tsp tomato purée

1 Heat half the olive oil in a dish on HIGH for 1 minute. Add the onion and garlic and cook for 3–4 minutes, stirring once.
2 Add the rest of the oil with the sliced peppers and cook for 4 minutes.
3 Pour boiling water over the tomatoes in a bowl, leave to stand for a few seconds and then slide off the skins. Chop the tomatoes roughly and drain off a little of the juice. Cook the tomatoes with the peppers on HIGH for 2 minutes.
4 Season with sugar, salt and pepper and stir in the tomato purée and cook again for 4–6 minutes.
5 Leave to cool and serve with hot rolls or French bread.

Pepper ring flowers (see p.20); Warm tomatoes with mozzarella (see p. 17); Peperonata.

Pepper ring 'flowers'

Cookery writers divide into two teams on the subject of decoration: the 'radish rose and tomato lily' artists and the simple 'no-nonsense' brigade. Choose for yourself what you want to do with this new variation on cream cheese and peppers.

2 firm red peppers, deseeded and cut into rings
225 g/8 oz curd cheese
2 egg yolks
salt and pepper
100 g–175 g/4–6 oz mixed cooked vegetables,
such as broccoli or cauliflower florets, peas,
radishes, asparagus tips
Decoration
lettuce leaves
10 cm/4 in piece cucumber
sprigs of chervil or dill

1 Arrange half the pepper rings round a shallow flat dish. Cook on HIGH for 1 minute.
2 Mix the curd cheese with the egg yolks and season lightly. Spoon some of the mixture into each pepper ring and flatten the top.
3 Arrange some cooked vegetables on top of the cheese mixture, press down slightly and cook for just over a minute or until the mixture is slightly set. Repeat with the rest of the pepper rings and cheese. Leave to cool.
4 When cold, lift off the rings with a spatula or palette knife on to individual plates. Then either decorate with a few lettuce leaves and thin cucumber slices or make 'flowers' with cucumber skin stems and either chervil or dill leaves.
5 Serve with Tomato Vinaigrette (see p. 41) or Pepper Coulis (see p. 37)

Almond, onion and mushroom pâté

Cooking onions in a microwave has two advantages – you can't burn them if you turn your back, and your hair won't smell when you've finished! However, to bring about the sweet transformation from the raw state, you must cook them in either oil or butter, make sure they are soft and season well after cooking.

25 g/1 oz salted butter
½ large Spanish onion, finely chopped
75 g/3 oz flat mushrooms, finely chopped
salt and pepper
2 tbsp chopped fresh parsley
50 g/2 oz ground almonds
To serve
Melba toast
Yogurt and Herb Dip (see p. 41) or
*   smatana*

1 Melt half the butter in a dish on HIGH for about 40 seconds. Stir in the onion and cook for 2 minutes. Stir and cook for another 30 seconds.
2 Add the rest of the butter and the mushrooms and cook on HIGH for 2 minutes.
3 Stir again, season to taste and then mix in the parsley and almonds.
4 Spoon the pâté into four 50 ml/2 fl oz ramekins and level the tops. Leave to cool.
5 Run a knife round the edges and turn out on to plates. Serve with Melba toast and yogurt and herb dip or smatana.

Courgettes in fresh tomato sauce

Most good cooks rave about basil but I had never liked it until I spent a holiday in Sicily. There they sprinkle it on everything – pizzas, salads, charcoal-grilled fish and especially tomatoes. The southern plants have very small leaves and this probably accounts for the less pungent flavour which converted me.

450 g/1 lb courgettes, sliced
1 tbsp oil
Sauce
350 g/12 oz very ripe tomatoes (about 4)
1 tbsp olive oil
1 onion, finely chopped
½ tsp sugar
salt and pepper
2 tsp tomato purée (optional)
few leaves fresh basil, chopped

1 To make the sauce, immerse the tomatoes in boiling water for a few seconds, until the skin peels off easily. Chop them roughly.
2 Heat the olive oil in a dish on HIGH for about 50 seconds and stir in the onion. Cook for 3 minutes, stirring once, until the onion has softened.
3 Add the chopped tomatoes with their juice, the sugar and salt and pepper and cook for another 3 minutes.
4 Leave to cool slightly, then sieve the sauce into a bowl. Test the seasoning and add the tomato purée if the taste is not strong enough (this depends very much on the natural flavour of the tomatoes). Stir in a little chopped basil and reserve the rest to sprinkle over the top.
5 Heat the oil on HIGH for 40 seconds, add the courgettes and cook on HIGH for about 4 minutes, stirring once. Pour over the tomato sauce and leave to cool. Sprinkle with the reserved basil just before serving.

Taramosalata with cucumber

The authentic Greek version of this fish roe pâté uses 450 ml/¾ pint olive oil. Though I have unashamedly left most of it out, this version still tastes more like the real thing than the pink mixture you buy in supermarkets. The cooked cucumber is a good contrast to the salty cod's roe.

275 g/10 oz cucumber
salt and pepper
100 g/4 oz smoked cod's roe
1 slice white bread, 5 cm/2 in thick
juice of 1 lemon
3 tbsp olive oil
To serve
black olives
pitta bread

1 Peel the cucumber and cut it lengthwise into sticks. Remove the centre portion which is mainly seeds and cut the rest into cubes. Leave to drain for a few minutes on absorbent kitchen paper.
2 Transfer the cucumber to a dish and cook on HIGH, covered, for 2 minutes, then season lightly.
3 Split open the cod's roe, place in a dish, cover with 2 tbsp boiling water and cook on HIGH for 40 seconds. Remove the skin and drain if necessary.
4 Soak the bread in cold water and immediately squeeze it dry.
5 In a food processor or blender, process the cod's roe with the bread, alternately adding the lemon juice and the oil. Process until it is smooth.
6 Arrange the taramosalata in the centre of the plates, surrounded by the cucumber cubes. Serve with black olives and warm pitta bread.

Brioches with creamed mushrooms

If you've invited a friend and are worried about what to make, walk past the ready-cooked dishes in the supermarket and try this instead. The faint sweetness of brioche buns filled with a rich mushroom sauce could be followed by lemony grilled fish or barbecued steak. To complete the meal, serve a tossed green salad and a bowl of fresh berries.

300 ml/½ pint Béchamel Sauce (see p.32)
25 g/1 oz salted butter
350 g/12 oz mushrooms
black pepper
2 tsp dry sherry
2 tsp naturally fermented soy sauce
4 French brioche buns

1 First make the béchamel sauce.
2 Melt the butter in a dish on HIGH for 40 seconds. Stir in the sliced mushrooms and cook for 2 minutes until the juices start to run. Season with pepper.
3 Preheat the conventional grill.
4 Mix the mushrooms with the sauce, then add the sherry and soy sauce. Taste for seasoning, then cook on HIGH for 30 seconds. Turn to KEEP WARM setting and leave for 5 minutes.
5 Split the brioches in half horizontally and scoop out some of the soft cakey centre. Place the opened halves under the grill and heat through until the edges are crisp and the centres warm. Be careful not to burn them.
6 Spoon the hot mushroom mixture into the brioches, cover with the tops and arrange on individual plates.

Mushroom risotto (see p. 25); Brioche with creamed mushrooms; Vegetable tartlets with peas and carrots (see p. 28).

Spanish bean, asparagus and egg salad

Here's a recipe dedicated to all those who are trying to lose weight and can't! It's an appetizing salad with no dressing or sauce at all.

225 g/8 oz curly Spanish beans
225 g/8 oz asparagus tips
3 hard-boiled eggs
3 spring onions, sliced
4 radishes, diced
5 cm/2 in piece of cucumber, diced
salt and pepper
12 cherry tomatoes, to serve (optional)

1 Top and tail the beans and cut them into 7.5 cm/3 in lengths. Discard the tough ends of the asparagus and cut the tips into 5 cm/2 in lengths.
2 Put the beans in a dish, sprinkle with 2 tbsp salted water, cover and cook on HIGH for 4 minutes.
3 Cook the asparagus tips and pieces in the same amount of water for 4 minutes. Drain both the vegetables and leave to cool.
4 Chop or grate the hard-boiled eggs and mix with the onions, radishes and cucumber. Mix them all together and season lightly.
5 Arrange the egg salad in the centre of individual plates with a border of the beans and asparagus tips. Add some cherry tomatoes if they are available.

Note: Spanish beans are flat runner beans with wavy sides. Unlike the straight-sided English runner beans they are not stringy so you only have to cut off the ends.

Leeks with red pepper rings

Leeks vary enormously in size. Sometimes three large ones will weigh the same as fourteen small ones. The dark green ends are tough, so you should use mainly the white parts and keep the thick, greenish bits for soup.

700 g/1½ lb small leeks
3–4 tbsp chicken or vegetable stock
1–2 tsp olive oil
225 g/8 oz red peppers, deseeded and cut into rings
salt and black pepper
Walnut Vinaigrette (see p. 16)

1 Wash the leeks very well, making sure there is no grit inside (split larger ones horizontally as it makes them easier to clean). Trim into even lengths and drain well.
2 Put the leeks in a dish with the stock, cover and cook on HIGH for 4–6 minutes. Leave to stand for 1–2 minutes – they should be tender but not too soft. Drain and keep the stock for another use.
3 Heat the oil in a dish on HIGH for about 30 seconds, add the pepper rings and toss to coat with the oil. Cook for 2 minutes until they are slightly wilted but still a little crisp. Season and leave to cool.
4 Arrange the leeks in a circle with the peppers in the centre. Sprinkle over a little vinaigrette and serve the rest separately. This salad is best cool, but not chilled.

Mushroom risotto

Dried Italian mushrooms (porcini) are an expensive delicacy, but you only need a few to add a strong flavour.

25 g/1 oz porcini
225 g/8 oz Italian brown rice
40 g/1½ oz butter
225 g/8 oz fresh mushrooms, sliced
1 tbsp lemon juice
salt and pepper
300 ml/½ pint Vegetable Stock (see p. 44)
To serve
chopped flat-leaf parsley
freshly grated Parmesan cheese

1 Heat 125 ml/4 fl oz water in a glass for about 40 seconds on HIGH, drop in the porcini and leave them to soak for about 30 minutes, pushing them down occasionally. Remove the porcini, strain the juice carefully through muslin or a coffee filter and reserve it. Wash the porcini in cold water to remove any grit and dry well. Chop them roughly.
2 Put the rice in a large casserole, cover with 575 ml/1 pint boiling water and cook on HIGH for 10 minutes. Drain, then rinse the rice in cold running water.
3 Heat half the butter in a dish on HIGH for 45 seconds, add the fresh mushrooms and cook for 2 minutes. Stir in the lemon juice and season well.
4 Heat the remaining butter on HIGH for 45 seconds, stir in the rice with the juices from the porcini and the mushrooms. Add the chopped porcini and the vegetable stock and cook on HIGH for about 5 minutes to bring back to the boil. Stir and continue cooking for another 5 minutes. Add the mushroom slices and cook for another 2 minutes, by which time most of the stock will have been absorbed. Stir again and leave covered for about 5 minutes.

5 Serve the risotto on warmed plates, sprinkled with chopped parsley and plenty of grated Parmesan cheese.

Note: this makes enough for 4 small portions as it is quite a filling starter. If you increase the quantities, allow longer cooking times.

Smoked salmon with asparagus tips

The best advice about choosing canned artichokes is 'don't' and the same applies to asparagus. For this recipe you only need the tips, but don't discard the rest because you can use them another time for soup.

700 g/1½ lb thick, short asparagus (about 20)
275 g/10 oz smoked Scotch salmon (see note below)
1 large lemon
thinly sliced wholemeal bread and butter, to serve

1 Prepare the asparagus and cook in 2 batches (see p. 16) on HIGH for about 5 minutes. The tips should be just tender but not limp.
2 Spread out the smoked salmon and cut it into even strips about 10 x 2.5 cm (4 x 1 in), there should be about 20.
3 Drain the asparagus, and cut the tips into even lengths and leave to cool. Meanwhile, prepare the bread and butter and keep covered with clingfilm.
4 Roll up the asparagus in the smoked salmon strips. Arrange 5 asparagus rolls on each plate in a fan shape. Divide the lemon into 4 and place a quarter on the side of each serving.

Note: You may need to buy 450 g/1 lb smoked salmon as there is some waste when you cut it into neat strips. Any remaining pieces can be used in sandwiches.

Avocado and broad bean salad

Both avocados and broad beans are acquired tastes – here they are together in a starter that would go well with fish.

700 g/1½ lb broad beans in their pods
4 tbsp vegetable stock or water
salt and pepper
120 ml/4 fl oz soured cream or smatana
2 large ripe avocados
juice of ½ lemon
2 tbsp hazelnut oil
1 tsp wine vinegar
50 g/2 oz toasted chopped hazelnuts

1 Shell the beans and put in a dish with the stock. Cover and cook on HIGH for 5 minutes. When they have cooled slightly, remove the skins if they are tough. Season.
2 Mix the beans with the soured cream or smatana.
3 Peel and halve the avocados, then slice them lengthwise and brush with the lemon juice. Mix together the oil, vinegar and seasoning; sprinkle this dressing over the pears just before serving.
4 Arrange 4 plates with a pile of the bean mixture and the sliced avocados. Shake the hazelnuts over the broad beans and serve immediately.

Leeks with red pepper rings (see p. 24); Avocado and broad bean salad.

Vegetable tartlets with peas and carrots

Frozen vegetables are generally not as good as freshly picked ones. However, the freezing process of peas, using the pick of the crop, means that the smallest and sweetest ones now come in packets rather than pods. These tartlets have a filling of mascarpone cheese – a semi-sweet Italian cream cheese. To counteract this, the carrots have a lemon glaze.

Pastry
150 g/5 oz butter
225 g/8 oz plain flour
1 egg yolk
4 tbsp cold water
Filling
2 carrots
2 tbsp strong vegetable stock
100 g/4 oz frozen peas
100 g/4 oz mascarpone cheese
Glaze
1 tsp powdered gelatine
3 tbsp lemon juice

1 First make the pastry. Rub the butter into the flour and mix to a dough with the egg yolk and water. Chill in the refrigerator if it is too soft to handle. Roll out the pastry very thinly and lift it carefully with a palette knife over some small tartlet tins. (This amount of pastry is enough for about 22 tartlets but you only need 12 for this recipe. Store the remainder cooked or uncooked in the freezer.)
2 Press the rolling pin forward over the tops, cutting off each one. Push the pastry into the tartlet tins, pricking the bases and pressing the edges with a fork. Bake in a preheated oven at 220 C (425 F/Gas 7) for about 10 minutes or until they are brown. When they are cooked they will slip easily out of the tins. Leave to cool.
3 Cut the carrots into round slices and, if you like, into decorative shapes. Put in a dish with the stock, cover and cook on HIGH for 1–2 minutes. Leave to cool.
4 Cook the peas on HIGH, with no liquid, for 2 minutes. Season and cool.
5 To make the glaze, mix the gelatine with the lemon juice and cook on HIGH for 30 seconds. Leave to cool slightly.
6 Spread a spoonful of the cream cheese into each tartlet and arrange the carrots and peas over the top. Brush the lemon glaze over the carrots (not the peas or they will discolour).

Note: These tartlets are good with drinks. They can be prepared up to an hour in advance and left in a cool place, but not the refrigerator. A sprig of chervil makes a pretty garnish.

Blue brie pancakes with sliced avocado and tomato sauce

It is impossible to make pancakes in the microwave, but you can reheat the filled pancakes without melting the cheese inside. Everything is prepared in advance, except for the sliced avocados. It's a good idea to buy an extra avocado in case one of them turns out to be black or over-ripe when you cut it open.

Pancakes
100 g/4 oz plain flour
pinch salt
1 egg
300 ml/½ pint milk
1 tsp oil (plus more for frying)
225 g/8 oz blue brie cheese, chilled
2 avocados
1 tbsp walnut oil
1 tsp wine vinegar
Tomato Sauce
4 peeled plum tomatoes, drained well if canned
2 tsp tomato purée
¼ tsp sugar
salt and pepper
pinch oregano

1 To make the pancake batter, sift the flour and salt into a bowl and make a well in the centre. Add the egg, then gradually beat in the milk and oil, drawing in the flour to make a smooth batter.
2 Heat a little oil in a frying pan until very hot. Pour in enough batter to cover the base of the pan and cook over high heat until golden brown, then turn over and cook the other side. Repeat with the remaining batter to make 8 pancakes. Separate the stacked, fried pancakes with greaseproof paper. (You can do this the day before or freeze them).
3 To make the sauce, put the tomatoes into a small bowl. Mash them roughly and stir in the tomato purée, sugar, salt, pepper and oregano. Cover and cook on HIGH for 1½

minutes. Leave to cool slightly, then press through a strainer into a jug.
4 Remove the hard crust from the brie. Cut the cheese into cubes and divide it into 8. Lay out the pancakes with a line of cheese cubes along one edge. Roll them up and fold in the sides, making sure the cheese is totally enclosed. Arrange them close together in a single layer in a dish. Cook, uncovered, on HIGH for 2½–3 minutes, or until the pancakes are hot.
5 Meanwhile, peel and slice the avocados and sprinkle over the walnut oil and vinegar.
6 Arrange the hot pancakes on large plates with a spoonful of sauce at the side and the sliced, drained avocados arranged in a fan.

Sugar peas with hollandaise sauce

Few vegetables can stand alone as a first course. Sugar peas are rounder than mange-tout but sweet enough to eat whole. They should be lightly cooked so they stay crisp, and need only some lemony hollandaise to bring them into the asparagus class.

450 g/1 lb sugar peas
salt and pepper
To serve
Hollandaise Sauce (see p. 32)
crunchy bread

1 Top and tail the sugar peas, removing any stringy bits at the sides. Rinse in cold water and arrange in a single layer in a dish. Sprinkle over 2 tbsp water, cover and cook on HIGH for 4 minutes.
2 Sprinkle the sugar peas with salt and pepper, toss and then drain.
3 Pile them on to warmed plates and serve with small individual pots of hollandaise sauce and crunchy bread.

Sauces and Dips

A young student, who later turned out to be an excellent cook, once found a recipe for a dish called Gado Gado. He spent hours preparing a dozen different vegetables and even longer making the peanut sauce to go over them. The sauce tasted ghastly, so in desperation he drained it all off and liquidized the vegetables, turning them into a slightly less disgusting soup! The moral of this tale is that you can ruin anything with a bad sauce. There are no such problems with these sauces – they are not meant to drown the taste of the vegetables, but should help to bring out the flavours. A squeeze of lemon juice, some chopped herbs, a knob of butter or a dash of wine will transform a plain dish into a masterpiece.

People often complain that there isn't much point in microwaving sauces as you still have to open the door to stir them. This is true, but no-one ever said you had to forget your cooking skills when you bought your microwave cooker. It will save you the trouble of using double saucepans since you can whisk up a small quantity of sauce in a pretty jug or bowl, ready to bring to the table the moment it is cooked.

Hollandaise sauce

Pastry, soufflés and hollandaise sauce – the beginner's nightmares! There is no mystique about the sauce – it's just a matter of pouring hot melted butter on to egg yolks to form an emulsion, rather like hot mayonnaise. The only thing to remember is that you must keep stirring otherwise it might curdle.

100 g/4 oz salted butter
2 large egg yolks
1 tbsp lemon juice
1 tbsp wine vinegar
pepper
2 tsp boiling water

1 Put the butter in a jug and cook on HIGH for about 1 minute to melt.
2 Mix the egg yolks, lemon juice and vinegar together in a 175 ml/6 fl oz capacity sauceboat, then pour on the melted butter, whisking well.
3 Cook on LOW for 50 seconds, stirring frequently, until the sauce just begins to thicken. It will continue to cook and thicken more after it is removed from the microwave.
4 Season with pepper and stir in the boiling water, then serve immediately.

Béchamel sauce

Using a jug saves sticky pans, but only frequent stirring will give you this smooth, traditional base for many classic sauces.

25 g/1 oz butter
25 g/1 oz flour
3 tbsp vegetable stock and
*   300 ml/½ pint milk (or all milk)*
salt and pepper

1 Put the butter in a jug and cook on HIGH for 40 seconds.
2 Stir in the flour and the vegetable stock (or 3 tbsp milk if using all milk), to make a smooth paste. Add one-third of the milk and cook for 1 minute.
3 Stir very well, add more milk and cook for another 30 seconds. Continue opening the door to stir in the milk until the sauce is thick. This should take 2 or 3 minutes altogether.
4 Season with salt and pepper.

Cheese sauce

300 ml/½ pint Béchamel Sauce (see above)
50–75 g/2–3 oz mature Cheddar, Gruyère or
*   fresh Parmesan cheese, grated*
salt and pepper

1 Make the béchamel sauce.
2 Stir in the grated cheese and cook on LOW for about 30 seconds, or until it is melted. Stir the sauce and taste for seasoning.

Wine and cream sauce

This is a variation of béchamel sauce that is excellent with either fish or vegetables.

25 g/1 oz butter
25 g/1 oz flour
25 ml/1 fl oz dry white wine
75 ml/3 fl oz vegetable or fish stock (see note below)
salt and pepper
50 ml/2 fl oz whipping cream, fresh or frozen

1 Put the butter in a jug and cook on HIGH for 40 seconds. Mix in the flour and wine to make a smooth paste.
2 Heat the stock on HIGH for 30 seconds, stir it into the paste, then cook on HIGH, stirring frequently for about 2–3 minutes, or until the sauce has thickened.
3 Season to taste, then beat in the cream. (If it is frozen the heat of the sauce will melt it quickly.) Taste again and adjust the seasoning if necessary, then serve hot.

Note: You can make and freeze fish stock easily. Boil up the trimmings from salmon or other fish with enough water to cover. Simmer for about 15 minutes, strain and leave to cool.

Mushroom sauce

300 ml/½ pint Béchamel Sauce (see opposite)
25 g/1 oz salted butter
350 g/12 oz flat or dark mushrooms, sliced
salt and pepper
pinch grated nutmeg
3 tbsp single cream (optional)

1 Make the béchamel sauce. Put the butter in a bowl and cook on HIGH for 40 seconds to melt.
2 Mix in the mushrooms and cook for 2 minutes, stirring once.
3 Pour the cooked mushrooms with their juice into the béchamel sauce and season with salt, pepper and nutmeg.
4 Purée the sauce in a blender or food processor (the blender will give a more velvety consistency) and stir in the single cream if using.

Lemon sauce

Broccoli, courgettes or artichokes go particularly well with this fresh-tasting sauce; have them cooked and hot for when the sauce is ready. They are best served as a course on their own – rather than battling with the stronger flavours of fish or meat.

2 egg yolks
juice of ½ lemon
75 ml/3 fl oz light Chicken Stock, slightly warmed (see p. 44)

1 Mix the egg yolks with the lemon juice in a jug and stir in the stock. Cook on MEDIUM for 1 minute. Stir and cook for another minute, stopping once or twice to stir again to make sure the sauce does not curdle. It will thicken slightly as it heats.
2 Leave the sauce to stand for a few minutes, then pour over the vegetables and serve immediately.

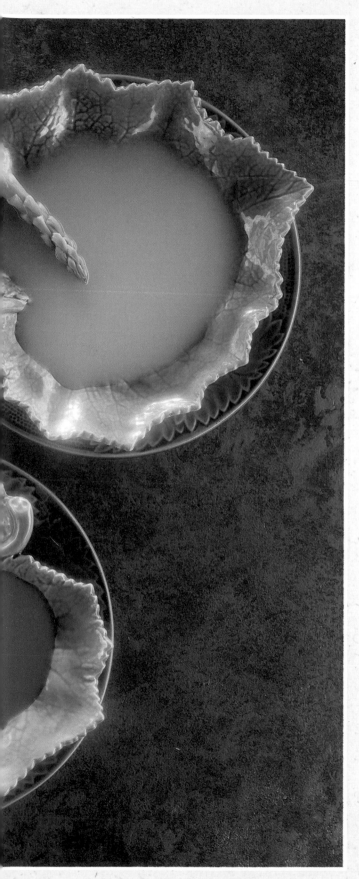

Aubergine dip

In Italian markets you can find piles of shiny, round aubergines with white and violet tops. Cooked aubergines often have a rather disappointing muddy colour, but this dip is a delicate pale green due to the greatly reduced cooking time.

2 aubergines
3–4 tbsp olive oil
2 cloves garlic, crushed
½ onion, chopped
juice of ½ lemon
pinch sugar
salt and pepper
To serve
pitta bread and black olives or sticks of raw vegetable crudités

1 Prick the aubergines in several places and cook on HIGH for 4–6 minutes until they are soft.
2 Put 1 tbsp oil in a dish and cook on HIGH for 30 seconds, then add the garlic and onion and cook for 2–3 minutes, stirring occasionally.
3 Cut the aubergines in half and scoop out the seeds. Scrape out all the flesh and purée it in a blender or food processor with the lemon juice.
4 Add the garlic, onion and sugar, season well and blend, gradually adding the rest of the oil until you have a fairly thick, pale purée.
5 Cool quickly, then cover with clingfilm to stop it discolouring until ready to serve.

Aubergine dip; Red and yellow pepper coulis (see p. 37).

Watercress purée

This fresh, green sauce is good with fish and spinach. Don't be tempted to use tired and yellowing watercress just because you are going to purée it.

1 bunch watercress
50 ml/2 fl oz vegetable stock
50 ml/2 fl oz fresh cream
salt and pepper

1 Discard the stalks and wash the watercress well. Shake off the surplus water and dry with absorbent kitchen paper.
2 Put the watercress in a bowl, cover and cook on HIGH for 1 minute. In a separate bowl, cook the stock for 1 minute.
3 Pour the hot vegetable stock into a blender and add the watercress. Blend until it is smooth, then pour in the cream and season with salt and pepper. Serve immediately or keep warm on DEFROST setting.

Smatana with chives

Butter has an affinity with hot vegetables and soured cream with cold ones. Low-fat yogurt is easy to get but rather tart. Greek yogurt is better, but best of all – and cheaper – is thick, creamy smatana. This sauce is specially good with jacket potatoes.

300 ml/½ pint creamed smatana
handful of fresh chives or finely chopped spring
  onion tops

Mix the smatana with the chives and spoon into a bowl. Leave, covered, in the refrigerator for the flavour to develop. Serve cool with hot vegetables.

Tomato sauce

What's the advantage of making a sauce like this in the microwave? Speed of course, but it also makes it easier. There will be no smell of frying onions and as you make it in a covered earthenware pot, there's no saucepan or hob to clean afterwards.

2 tbsp sunflower oil
1 onion, finely chopped
1 clove garlic, crushed
salt and pepper
500 g/1¼ lb carton Italian creamed tomatoes or
  2 x 400 g/14 oz cans tomatoes, drained and
  mashed
½ tsp sugar
1–2 tbsp chopped fresh oregano or ½ tsp dried
  oregano

1 Pour half the oil into a heavy 600 ml/1 pint casserole and cook on HIGH for 1 minute.
2 Add the onion and garlic and stir to coat with the oil. Cook on HIGH for 2 minutes, adding the rest of the oil and stirring halfway through. Cook for a further 2 minutes to soften the onion, then sprinkle with salt and pepper.
3 Add the tomatoes and stir in more seasoning, the sugar and half the chopped oregano.
4 Cover and cook on HIGH for 3 minutes. Stir again, then serve sprinkled with the rest of the oregano.

Celeriac sauce

If you are looking for an alternative to a rich cream sauce, try this simple vegetable purée. Celeriac looks like a turnip but has a much more subtle flavour that goes well with plain or stuffed vegetables.

1 lemon
275 g/10 oz celeriac
1 tbsp oil
1 small onion, finely chopped
175 ml/6 fl oz Light Vegetable Stock (see p. 44)
salt and pepper
1/2 tsp freshly grated nutmeg

1 Grate the lemon rind and set it aside. Cut the lemon in half and squeeze half of it into a bowl filled with cold water, dropping the squeezed half in as well.
2 Cut the celeriac into quarters, remove and discard the spongy centre and peel the rest, making sure you remove all the brown parts. Chop the celeriac into fairly small pieces and immediately drop them into the acidulated water.
3 Heat the oil in a dish on HIGH for 40 seconds, add the onion and cook for 2–3 minutes, stirring occasionally, until soft.
4 Drain the celeriac and put in a dish with half the stock, cover and cook on HIGH for about 5 minutes, or until soft, then purée it in a blender with the onion, rest of the stock, salt, pepper, grated nutmeg and lemon rind. Add the juice from the remaining half of the lemon and taste for seasoning. If the purée is too thick, add a little extra stock. Reheat gently and stir before serving.

Red or yellow pepper coulis

Peppers come in all shades of colours, ranging in ripeness between green, orangy green, yellow, true orange and red. You can even get gimmicky black varieties but for a naturally sweet sauce it's best to avoid these. Old-fashioned methods of charring under a grill, or sautéeing in a pan, dull the finished purée. The microwave is used here not for speed but to retain the brilliant colours.

2 red or yellow peppers, deseeded
1–2 tbsp oil
about 2 tbsp vegetable stock or water
salt and pepper

1 Cut the peppers into strips.
2 Heat the oil in a shallow dish on HIGH for about 40 seconds and then add the red or yellow peppers. (If you want 1 red and 1 yellow sauce, cook the peppers separately.) Cook on HIGH for about 3 minutes, stirring occasionally.
3 Moisten with the stock or water and cook for a further 1–2 minutes.
4 Purée the peppers in a blender or food processor and then press through a fine sieve to remove all the skin.
5 Stir the sauce well, adding a little more stock or water if it is too thick. Season to taste and leave to cool.

Green mayonnaise

The colour and flavour of this mayonnaise comes from the herbs and intensifies if you leave it for a while before serving.

1 whole egg
1 egg yolk
2 tbsp wine vinegar
salt and black pepper
¼ tsp made mustard
300 ml/½ pint olive or sunflower oil
½ bunch watercress
4–5 parsley sprigs
2 tbsp vinaigrette or boiling water

1 Put the eggs in a blender with the vinegar, salt, pepper and mustard. Process together on medium speed and start pouring in the oil in a slow, steady stream.
2 Increase the flow as the mayonnaise starts to thicken, but be careful not to add the oil too fast or it will curdle. When all the oil has been added the mayonnaise should be thick and creamy.
3 Scoop the mayonnaise into a bowl, using a plastic spatula.
4 Wash and dry the watercress and parsley and cut off the stalks and any yellowing leaves.
5 Process the herbs with the vinaigrette or water in the blender until they are very finely chopped. Spoon in some of the mayonnaise and continue processing until it is smooth and green. Gently fold in the rest and taste for seasoning.

Vegetable terrine with mousseline of fish (see p. 105) with Tomato vinaigrette (see p. 41); Baby artichokes (see p. 17) with Green mayonnaise and Hollandaise (see p. 32).

Apple and mint sauce

Apple sauce goes with duck and mint sauce (or jelly) with lamb. This combination makes a good accompaniment for both, or can be used to liven up an oily fish like mackerel. It makes enough for three small pots, which is useful as it freezes well.

450 g/1 lb cooking apples
7 g/¼ oz mint leaves (4 or 5 sprigs)
1 tbsp sugar
2 tbsp boiling water

1 Peel and core the apples and cut them into small pieces.
2 Wash the fresh mint and pat it dry with absorbent kitchen paper.
3 Put the apples into a bowl, sprinkle over the sugar and then add the mint. Pour over the boiling water, cover and cook on HIGH for 4 minutes. The apples should be soft and collapsed by this time.
4 Purée the apples and mint in a blender or food processor, then spoon the sauce into small pots. Leave to cool.

Cucumber sauce

This is a quick sauce which goes well with fish and vegetables – both raw and cooked. I have chosen as a base a fairly low-fat mixture of curd cheese and smatana, although you could substitute anything you prefer from the range of skimmed milk cheese, cream cheese or even mayonnaise.

150 g/5 oz cucumber
salt and pepper
2 large spring onions, sliced
140 g/4 ½ oz curd cheese
75 g/3 oz smatana

1 Chop the cucumber but don't peel it. Put in a dish, cover and cook on HIGH for 2 minutes. Season well with salt and pepper.
2 Add the sliced onions, using both the white and green parts and cook for 40 seconds.
3 Leave to cool slightly, then spoon the vegetables into a blender. Add half the curd cheese and process until the mixture is smooth. Add the remaining cheese and stir in the smatana. Taste again for seasoning, then cover and leave in the refrigerator for the flavours to develop.

Lemon mayonnaise

This recipe is the result of my experiment with a 'cooked' mayonnaise on the lines of a hollandaise sauce. Butter-based sauces are usually served hot, but this oil-based one is better when it is cold.

2 egg yolks
2 tbsp lemon juice
½ tbsp wine vinegar
salt and pepper
125 ml/4 fl oz olive oil

1 Whisk the egg yolks with 1 tbsp lemon juice and the wine vinegar in a bowl. Season lightly with salt and pepper.
2 Cook the oil in a jug on HIGH for about 30 seconds. Start pouring it, in a thin stream, on to the egg yolks, whisking vigorously. Continue adding the oil, whisking slowly all the time, until it forms an emulsion.
3 Cook the sauce on DEFROST (3) for 30 seconds. Stir well and continue for another minute, stirring 2 or 3 times until the mayonnaise is thick. Taste for seasoning, stir in the rest of the lemon juice and leave to cool.

Tomato vinaigrette

A thick, cool sauce for fish or vegetable terrines.

300 ml/½ pint creamed tomatoes or drained canned whole tomatoes
½ tsp sugar
½ tsp cayenne pepper or paprika (optional)
salt and pepper
2 tsp wine vinegar
50 ml/2 fl oz olive oil

1 Put the creamed or drained tomatoes into a blender with the sugar, cayenne or paprika, salt, pepper and the wine vinegar.
2 Start processing the tomato mixture and trickle in the oil, slowly, until you have a thick sauce.

Yogurt and herb dip

Thick Greek yogurt is less acid than ordinary low-fat yogurt. Don't worry if it seems to get thinner when you mix in the herbs. After the brief cooking it sets and the flavour develops as it cools.

3 tbsp Greek yogurt
1 tbsp chopped fresh chives
1 tbsp chopped fresh chervil or dill
1 egg yolk
salt and pepper

1 Mix the yogurt with the chopped herbs in a bowl and stir in the egg yolk and seasoning.
2 Cook on MEDIUM for about 3 minutes, stirring every 30 seconds to make sure it does not curdle.
3 Stand the bowl in cold water and leave to cool and thicken.

Soups

When I was a teenager I couldn't cook at all, although my mother was a wonderful pastry cook and her teas were famous for miles around. But I loved to try my hand at soups; they were the only things the rest of the family would allow me to touch since they believed that nothing really bad could happen to them. How right they were. There's no careful balance in weighing ingredients or immaculate timing to be considered. Soup making is fun and very individual – you just choose what you like, add a good stock and you can hardly go wrong. If you are new to cooking, soup must be the least worrying course you could choose for a dinner party. If you are an expert, it gives you a chance to concentrate on a more elaborate main course and dessert.

Most vegetable soups don't need a meat-based stock but sometimes you may want to strengthen the natural flavours. Soup cubes should be used sparingly, as they are full of salt and artificial ingredients and can be overpowering. For this reason it is worth making (and perhaps freezing) the light stock at the beginning of the chapter, as it can be cooking while you wash and prepare the other vegetables.

Light vegetable stock

You may prefer to make this stock in a saucepan or a pressure cooker. The result is the same but if you microwave it, you can concentrate on something else knowing it will switch itself off. Use other fresh vegetables of your choice if preferred: you need about 450 g/1 lb.

2 large carrots
2 onions
4 sticks celery
6 mushroom stalks
few sprigs parsley
salt and pepper
900 ml/1½ pints boiling water

1 Chop the vegetables finely with a knife or a food processor. Put them in a large casserole with the parsley, seasoning and one third of the boiling water. Cover and cook on HIGH for 10 minutes.
2 Add the rest of the water and cook on MEDIUM for 20–30 minutes. (The timing is not important but the taste improves if you leave the vegetables to infuse for longer.)
3 Strain the stock into a large jug, pressing down the vegetables to release all the juices.

Chicken stock

If you are not a vegetarian, you may want to add a good chicken stock to some of the soups. This is a microwave version of traditional Jewish chicken soup, using chicken pieces rather than a whole chicken. It's important to chill the stock thoroughly so that you can remove the fat from the top.

900 g/2 lb chicken pieces
1 small onion
1 large carrot
2 sticks celery
1.2 litres/2 pints boiling water
salt and pepper

1 Put the chicken pieces into a large casserole dish, add the vegetables and cover with the boiling water. Cook on HIGH for 10 minutes or until the water is boiling again. Season generously.
2 Skim the surface, cover and cook on LOW or SIMMER for about 1 hour.
3 Strain the stock, cool rapidly, chill or freeze until the fat is firm enough to remove.

Note: Use the cooked chicken in pancakes, risotto or in Leek and Chicken Soup with Corn (see p. 53)

Minestrone soup

You'll often find a large pot of minestrone or 'big soup' simmering on the hob in Italian homes. English mammas are more likely to be out working, so when they come home they need a quick version that can be cooked and served in the same tureen. The vegetables vary according to season – in winter leeks and celery can be used instead of courgettes and beans.

1 onion
2 carrots, trimmed
50 g/2 oz French beans, topped and tailed
50 g/2 oz runner beans, topped and tailed
50 g/2 oz courgettes, trimmed
40 g/1½ oz mushrooms
25 g/1 oz butter
900 ml/1½ pints boiling vegetable stock
25 g/1 oz tiny Italian soup pasta, such as stars
  or letters
freshly grated Parmesan cheese, to serve

1 Cut all the vegetables, separately, into small pieces, making sure they are all of a similar size.
2 Put half the butter in a very large tureen or casserole (it must be large or the soup might boil over) and cook on HIGH for 45 seconds. Add the onion, carrots and beans and cook for about 6 minutes, stirring to coat with the butter.
3 Add the courgettes, cook for 2 minutes, then add the rest of the butter with the mushrooms and cook for another 2 minutes.
4 Pour half the boiling stock and the pasta into the vegetable mixture. Cook for 5 minutes, stir in the rest of the stock and cook for a further 4 minutes or until the pasta and vegetables are tender.
5 Serve the soup with plenty of grated cheese sprinkled on the top.

Note: If the stock (or stock cube) is heavily seasoned you will not need any extra salt and pepper.

Corn and mushroom consommé

For this soup you need a really strong base – either a good beef or chicken stock, or a very well-flavoured vegetable one.

2 fresh corn cobs
900 ml/1½ pints well-flavoured stock
1 tbsp oil
5 large spring onions, finely chopped
150 g/5 oz small button mushrooms
salt and black pepper

1 Remove the leaves and silky strands and wash the corn cobs. Using a sharp knife, cut downwards to remove all the kernels.
2 Put them in a dish with 6 tbsp stock, cover and cook on HIGH for about 6 minutes, or until tender. (Very fresh corn takes less time to cook.)
3 In a separate dish, cook the oil on HIGH for 1 minute. Add the spring onions and the mushrooms and cook for 2–3 minutes.
4 Mix the vegetables together in a large casserole or bowl, season lightly and add the rest of the stock. Cover and cook on HIGH for about 8 minutes. Taste for seasoning. Serve the soup very hot in deep bowls.

Garden vegetable soup

Here's a quick lunchtime soup that needs no puréeing. If you like the Japanese style of decoratively cut vegetables, you can enjoy yourself with some tiny biscuit cutters. If not, an ordinary knife will do!

You use very little fat in this soup and can sauté one vegetable while you cut up another, with no danger of the first one burning while your back is turned. With the saucepan method, long simmering tends to dull the colours and there is the final worry that the velvety cream soup you left on the hob will have reduced to a sticky mess if your guests are late.

25 g/1 oz salted butter
100 g/4 oz carrots, diced or cut into shapes
100g/4 oz shelled fresh or frozen peas
4 or 5 spring onions, finely chopped
50 g/2 oz courgettes, sliced
25 g/1 oz mushrooms, sliced
300 ml/½ pint vegetable stock
300 ml/½ pint milk
salt and pepper

1 Put the butter in a large casserole and cook on HIGH for 50 seconds. Stir in the carrots, coating with the butter, add the fresh peas, if using, and cook on HIGH for 1 minute.
2 Add the spring onions and cook for 1 minute, then add the courgette and mushroom slices. Cook for another minute. Pour in the vegetable stock, cover and cook for 2 minutes. Add the milk and frozen peas, if using, and cook on MEDIUM for 5 minutes. Taste for seasoning and keep warm until you are ready to serve.

Note: This is one of the few soups which is good warm, not very hot.

Courgette and almond soup (see p. 48); Potato ball soup (see p. 49); Garden vegetable soup.

Courgette and almond soup

People used to cheat with drops of green food colouring to get an effect like this. The dark-edged courgette bows contrast with the pale soup and the toasted almonds add a little crunch to the smooth texture.

700 g/1½ lb courgettes, trimmed
600 ml/1 pint light vegetable stock
25 g/1 oz butter
1 large onion, chopped
salt and pepper
300 ml/½ pint milk
50 g/2 oz ground almonds
50 g/2 oz toasted slivered almonds
50 ml/2 fl oz single cream

1 Using a vegetable parer or potato peeler, cut enough courgettes lengthwise to make 12 long thin slivers. Push one end through a slit in the other end to make a bow, then cook the curled strips on HIGH for about 30 seconds.
2 Chop the remaining courgettes, removing some but not all of the skin, then put in a bowl with 150 ml/¼ pt stock, cover and cook on HIGH for 6 minutes. Leave to stand while preparing the onion.
3 Put the butter in a bowl and cook on high for about 40 seconds to melt. Add the onion and cook for 4–6 minutes, until soft, stirring occasionally to make sure it is well coated. Season with salt and pepper.
4 Purée the chopped courgettes with the onion, milk and ground almonds, adding enough stock to make a smooth soup. Taste for seasoning. Heat the soup bowls and have ready the almonds and cream.
5 Pour into bowls, swirl in the cream and then sprinkle over the toasted almonds and courgette bows.

Parsnip and mushroom soup

Root vegetables – though bland on their own – are good thickeners for soup. Adding nutmeg or stronger spices brings out the flavour of the warm and filling purée.

225 g/8 oz parsnips, thinly sliced
450 ml/¾ pint chicken or strong vegetable stock
25 g/1 oz butter
350 g/12 oz mushrooms, sliced
salt and pepper
¼ tsp cumin
½ tsp freshly grated nutmeg
150 ml/¼ pint milk

1 Put the parsnips in a bowl with 4 tbsp stock, cover and cook on HIGH for 5 minutes, or until soft.
2 Melt the butter in a large casserole on HIGH for 50 seconds, then add the sliced mushrooms. Cook on HIGH for 3 minutes, or until the juices begin to run. Season with salt and pepper.
3 Purée the vegetables with the rest of the stock, add the cumin and half the nutmeg and taste for seasoning. Add the milk and process until the soup is very smooth.
4 Reheat gently on LOW and sprinkle with the rest of the grated nutmeg.

Note: The consistency of soup is very much a matter of taste – personally I prefer it to be either very smooth or totally clear and I have never been very successful with the lumpy creations of my food processor. You will do far better with an old-fashioned 'mouli-légumes' or a blender. In some cases you may like to add more liquid than I have suggested, if you like a thinner soup.

Potato ball soup

This is a creamy soup using vegetables in two ways – for thickening and for garnishing.

700 g/1½ lb large potatoes
225 g/8 oz carrots
1 bunch spring onions
few cauliflower florets or celery sticks
75 ml/3 fl oz boiling water
salt and pepper
450 ml/¾ pint vegetable stock
15 g/½ oz butter
300 ml/½ pint milk

1 Using a melon/potato baller cut out balls from the potatoes and drop them, with the remaining part of the potatoes, into cold water. Cut the carrots into fine sticks. Finely chop the spring onions and roughly chop the cauliflower or celery.
2 Put the potato balls in a bowl with the boiling water and cook on HIGH for 4 minutes, or until just tender. Drain and season well.
3 Put the rest of the potatoes with the cauliflower or celery and half the carrot sticks in a dish with 150 ml/¼ pint vegetable stock and cook on HIGH for 5 minutes. When the vegetables are soft, put them in a blender with the rest of the stock and blend until they are smooth.
4 In a separate bowl, heat the butter on HIGH for 40 seconds, add the chopped onions and the rest of the carrot sticks and cook for 3 minutes.
5 Mix these with the cooked potato balls, pour over the soup purée and stir in the milk. Reheat the soup gently, taste for seasoning, and serve hot.

Note: You can keep this soup warm on a low setting.

Chilled onion soup

Here's a soup for one of those days when you have nothing in the refrigerator – it's what I call 'storecupboard food', invented on a Sunday night. Just this once you could even use a stock cube!

2 large onions, finely chopped
600 ml/1 pint vegetable or chicken stock
½ tsp sugar
salt and pepper
5 lettuce leaves, chopped
4 cooked potatoes
5 sticks frozen whipping cream thawed, or 150 ml/¼ pint fresh cream (see note below)
2 spring onions

1 Put the onions in a bowl with enough stock to cover the base of the container, cover and cook on HIGH for 7 minutes. Sprinkle with sugar and salt.
2 Add the lettuce leaves and cook for 2 minutes.
3 Pour half the remaining stock into a blender, add the onions and lettuce and the potatoes and blend for a few seconds. Add the rest of the stock and continue blending until the soup is smooth. Taste for seasoning.
4 Stir half the cream into the soup, then leave to cool. Serve with the chopped spring onions and the rest of the cream swirled over the top.

Note: It is a good idea to keep a bag of cream sticks in your freezer. They can be stirred, frozen, into hot soups or used to add richness to sauces.

Fresh pea soup with mint

Although peas in the pod come in uneven sizes and are not always quite as tender as frozen ones, the taste of fresh ones is incomparable. To make this soup you just need to add some fresh mint and really good stock.

1 kg/2¼ lb fresh peas in their pods (450 g/1 lb
  shelled)
10–12 mint sprigs
salt and pepper
1 tbsp oil
1 onion, finely chopped
800 ml/28 fl oz chicken, beef or vegetable stock

1 Shell the peas and put them in a pot with 200 ml/7 fl oz water and the sprigs of mint. Cover and cook on HIGH for 7–9 minutes, or until the peas are tender. Season lightly.
2 Heat the oil on HIGH for 1 minute in a bowl, then add the onion and cook for 4 minutes, stirring once.
3 Reserve a few peas for garnishing, then purée the remainder with their cooking water but without the mint. Add the onion and the stock and continue blending until the soup is very smooth.
4 Serve very hot with fresh mint leaves and a few peas floating in each bowl.

Leek and cucumber soup

This pale jade soup is deliciously good for you! The cool taste of cucumber goes well with little sandwiches of smoked cod's roe. You could even do without the bread and spread the roe straight on to slices of cucumber or into sticks of celery.

450 g/1 lb leeks, sliced
225 g/8 oz potatoes, peeled and diced
500 ml/18 fl oz strong chicken or vegetable
  stock
salt and pepper
15 g/½ oz butter
1 cucumber
400 ml/14 fl oz milk
To serve
50 g/2 oz smoked cod's roe

1 Wash the leeks thoroughly to remove any traces of grit. Drain well.
2 Put the potatoes in a shallow dish with enough boiling water to come halfway up the sides. Cover and cook on HIGH for 5 minutes, or until soft, then drain.
3 Put the leeks in a dish with 120 ml/4 fl oz stock and cook on HIGH for 8–9 minutes, or until soft. Season with salt and pepper.
4 Purée the leeks with the potatoes and the rest of the stock in a blender.
5 Put the butter in a small bowl and cook on HIGH for 35 seconds to melt. Cut half the cucumber into dice, add to the butter and cook for about 1½ minutes.
6 Pour the leek mixture into a bowl, blend the cucumber with the milk and stir into the leek mixture. Taste for seasoning and add a little more liquid if the soup seems too thick.
7 Slice the rest of the cucumber and cut some of the slices into triangles. Float these on top of the soup. Spread the cod's roe over the remaining slices and serve with the soup.

Leek and cucumber soup; Fresh pea soup with mint.

Celery soup

There are only two main ingredients in this soup – but you have to get them both right! The stock must be really good and the purée should be strained to avoid any stringy bits of celery.

l head celery, about 450 g/1 lb
900 ml–1.2 litres/1½–2 pints Chicken Stock
  (see p. 44)
salt and pepper
paprika
Garlic Toast Rounds (see p. 61), to serve

1 Wash the celery very well and remove some of the tough outer leaves and stalks. Reserve the small centre stalks to serve raw and chop the rest of the celery roughly.
2 Put the celery in a dish, cover and cook on HIGH for about 6 minutes, then add 300 ml/½ pint stock. Re-cover and cook for 3–4 minutes, or until the celery is soft.
3 Pour the stock and celery pieces into a blender and process until smooth. Pass it through a strainer, then purée the pieces again with the rest of the stock. Strain again and press the purée through leaving only the fibrous part of the celery in the sieve.
4 Reheat the soup, season to taste with salt, pepper and paprika and serve very hot with the garlic toast rounds.

Cream of tomato soup

The texture of most canned vegetables is not good, but canned Italian tomatoes are the exception. They make wonderful soups and sauces. Add a generous spoonful of cream and Drambuie, and you turn everyday ingredients into a magical bisque!

3 carrots, roughly chopped
1 tbsp oil
3 small onions, roughly chopped
1 clove garlic, crushed
700 g/1½ lb canned tomatoes
3 tbsp tomato purée
¼ tsp sugar
salt and black pepper
Béchamel sauce
25 g/1 oz butter
25 g/1 oz plain flour
300 ml/½ pint milk
To serve
4 tsp Drambuie
125 ml/4 fl oz fresh cream, thawed if frozen

1 Put the carrots in a dish, cover and cook on HIGH for about 5 minutes, or until they start to soften.
2 In a separate bowl, heat the oil on HIGH for 1 minute, add the onions and cook for 3 minutes. Stir in the garlic and cook for another minute. Add the carrots, the tomatoes, slightly mashed, and the tomato purée and season well with the sugar, salt and pepper. Cook for a further 5 minutes.
3 Meanwhile, make a béchamel sauce with the butter, flour and milk (see p. 32) and cook until it thickens.
4 Purée the tomato mixture in a blender with the sauce, in 2 batches, until smooth, then taste again for seasoning.
5 Stir in the Drambuie. Reheat the soup until it is very hot and pour it into bowls. Swirl in large spoonfuls of the cream and serve immediately.

Sweet potato soup with chestnut mushrooms

This soup is the result of a surprise find at a large supermarket. The interesting variety of mushrooms seemed to complement the reputed chestnut flavour of West Indian sweet potatoes.

800 g/1 lb 12 oz sweet potatoes, thinly sliced
800 ml/28 fl oz light vegetable stock
40 g/1½ oz butter
2 onions, finely chopped
salt and pepper
225 g/8 oz chestnut mushrooms, sliced into rings
300 ml/½ pint milk or cream

1 Put the sweet potatoes in a dish with 120 ml/4 fl oz stock, cover and cook on HIGH for 6–8 minutes. When cooked they are soft and the colour will change to a brighter orange.
2 Put 25 g/1 oz of the butter in a bowl and cook on HIGH for 1 minute to melt. Add the onions and cook for 3 minutes until they are soft and transparent. Season well.
3 Melt the remaining butter in a separate bowl, add the mushrooms and cook on HIGH for 2–2 ½ minutes. Drain, reserving the juice.
4 Purée the sweet potatoes in a blender with the remaining stock, onions and mushroom juice, then stir in the milk or cream. (You may have to do this in 2 batches, depending on the size of your blender.) Taste again for seasoning and serve very hot with the mushroom rounds floating on the top.

Note: This makes enough for about 8 large bowls of soup. If you want to freeze some, you should prepare the sweet potato and onion purée and reheat it from frozen with freshly cooked mushroom slices and cream.

Leek and chicken soup with corn

This is a very filling soup so you will only need a light main course to follow it.

225 g/8 oz leeks, cut into thin slices
1 tbsp oil
1 litre/1¾ pints Chicken Stock (see p. 44)
75 g/3 oz cooked sweetcorn kernels
150 g/5 oz cooked chicken pieces
salt and pepper

1 Wash the leeks thoroughly, then drain well. Heat the oil in a bowl on HIGH for 1 minute, add the leeks and cook for 3 minutes. Pour in 450 ml/¾ pint of the stock and cook, uncovered, for about 5 minutes, or until the leeks are tender.
2 Reserve a few rings and put the rest, with the sweetcorn and remaining stock, into a blender. Process until the soup is smooth, then pass it through a strainer.
3 Cut the chicken into shreds, add it to the strained soup, season and reheat it gently. Float the leek rings over the top and serve very hot.

Mushroom velvet soup

When you reheat a thick soup it often sticks to the base of the pan. If you do it in a microwave you can relax over a couple of drinks and not give it another thought. Talking of drinks, remember there's no such thing as 'cooking sherry'. It's more a matter of whether you prefer sweet or dry; swirl in 1 or 2 spoonfuls of the best, with some cream.

1 tbsp oil
450 g/1 lb mushrooms, roughly sliced
25 g/1 oz butter
1 onion, chopped
25 g/1 oz plain flour
150 ml/¼ pint vegetable stock
350 ml/12 fl oz milk
salt and pepper
To serve
4 tbsp sherry
4 tbsp single cream

1 Heat the oil on HIGH for 40 seconds, then stir in the mushrooms. Cook for 2 minutes, or until the juices run.
2 In a separate bowl, cook the butter on HIGH for 30 seconds, stir in the onion and cook for 1 minute. Stir and cook for another minute, then mix in the flour. Gradually add half the stock and cook for 2–3 minutes, stirring until the mixture is thick.
3 Stir in the mushrooms and juice, then purée in a blender with the milk and remaining stock, until reduced to a thick, smooth soup. Season and cook for another 2 minutes.
4 To keep it warm until ready to serve, simmer on LOW for about 10 minutes.
5 Pour the soup into warmed bowls and swirl in a spoonful of sherry. Float the cream on the top and serve immediately.

Minestrone soup (see p. 45); Mushroom and mozzarella toasts for soup (see p. 61); Mushroom velvet soup.

Sorrel and pea soup

Sorrel is common in France and in restaurants but rarely found in English greengrocers. If you are lucky enough to grow it, you will need just a few handfuls of young leaves for this soup. Spinach is a perfectly acceptable substitute.

15 g/½ oz butter
4 spring onions, finely chopped
225 g/8 oz shelled peas
250 g/9 oz sorrel or spinach leaves
350 ml/12 fl oz chicken or vegetable stock
300 ml/½ pint milk
salt and pepper
toasted bread croûtons, to serve

1 Put the butter in a bowl and cook on HIGH for 40 seconds, then stir in the onions and peas. Cook for 2 minutes, then remove a few of the peas and reserve for garnishing.
2 Wash the sorrel or spinach, drain it well and chop roughly. Add it to the other vegetables with 3 tbsp stock and cook on HIGH for 3 minutes.
3 Pour the mixture into a blender with the rest of the stock and process until it is smooth. Add the milk, process again and season to taste.
4 Reheat the soup gently and serve with toasted croûtons and the reserved peas floating on the top.

Celeriac soup

Although it wouldn't win any prizes for appearance, celeriac has the excellent flavour of celery, without any of the stringiness. It makes a creamy white soup which can seem bland, so be as generous as you like with the spicing.

½ lemon
1 celeriac, about 500 g/1 lb 2 oz
1 tbsp oil
1 onion, finely chopped
about 450 ml/¾ pint Light Vegetable Stock
* (see p. 44)*
salt and black pepper
300 ml/½ pint milk
2.5 cm/1 in piece ginger root, peeled
½ tsp freshly grated nutmeg
¼ tsp ground cumin
¼ tsp paprika

1 Squeeze the lemon juice into a bowl of cold water. Peel the celeriac, removing any brown parts which are difficult to get at with a vegetable parer. Chop the celeriac into fairly small pieces, discard the spongy centre core, and immediately drop the pieces into the acidulated water.
2 In a bowl, heat the oil on HIGH for 1 minute, add the chopped onion and cook for 2–3 minutes, or until soft.
3 Drain the celeriac and put in a dish with 150 ml/¼ pint of the stock, cover and cook on HIGH for 7 minutes.
4 Purée the celeriac with the onion and the rest of the stock in a blender and season with salt and pepper.
5 Put the milk into a jug. Grate in the ginger root and nutmeg and add the cumin. Heat on HIGH for 1 minute, then pour the spiced milk into the blender with the celeriac purée. Blend again until the mixture is smooth, taste for seasoning and add a little more vegetable stock or milk if the soup is too thick.
6 Serve the soup very hot, sprinkled with paprika.

Gazpacho

There are countless variations of this chilled Spanish soup. The common factors are fresh tomatoes, olive oil and garlic. Some people serve little piles of cucumbers, bread croûtons and peppers with the soup – others just throw everything in (I once knew someone who just puréed a bowl of salad!). Cooking the garlic and the tomatoes is far from traditional but, unless you like the robust flavour of raw garlic, I think it improves the taste.

725 g/1 lb 10 oz fresh ripe tomatoes
3 tbsp olive oil
2 cloves garlic, crushed
5 cm/2 in piece cucumber, chopped
1 sweet red pepper, chopped
2 spring onions, chopped
150 ml/¼ pint tomato juice
4 ice cubes
salt and pepper
Optional extras:
1 tbsp wine vinegar
raw onion, chopped
black olives, chopped
green peppers, chopped
pinch cumin, paprika or cayenne

1 Put the tomatoes in a deep bowl and pour over some boiling water. Leave for a few minutes and then peel off the skins. Cut the tomatoes in half and remove the pips. Drain and reserve the juice.
2 Heat 1 tbsp oil in a bowl on HIGH for 1 minute, add the garlic and cook for 30 seconds. Stir in the chopped tomatoes and cook on HIGH for 2 minutes.
3 Purée the tomatoes and garlic with the cucumber, pepper and onions and then pour in the tomato juice and the ice cubes. Stir in the rest of the oil, taste for seasoning and leave to chill thoroughly. Stir in any of the optional extras if using, and add to the soup or serve as accompaniments.

Tomato and red pepper soup

This is a cool soup for the end of summer when peppers are cheap and English tomatoes are ripe and plentiful.

5 large tomatoes
1–2 tbsp oil
1 onion, chopped
450 g/1 lb red peppers, deseeded and sliced
2 tbsp tomato purée
450 ml/¾ pint vegetable stock
salt and pepper
1 tsp sugar
To serve
4 tbsp smatana or soured cream
paprika
dill sprigs (optional)

1 Peel the tomatoes (see p. 21) and chop them, reserving the juice.
2 Heat half the oil in a bowl on HIGH for 1 minute. Add the onion and cook, stirring once, for 3 minutes.
3 Add the rest of the oil, stir in the chopped peppers and cook on HIGH for 4 minutes. Stir in the tomatoes, tomato purée and a few tablespoons of stock and cook for 5 minutes. Season with salt, pepper and sugar.
4 Purée the mixture in a blender or press it through a mouli-légumes, slowly adding the rest of the stock. (If you use the blender method you will have to strain the soup to remove the pepper skins.)
5 Taste again for seasoning and leave the soup to cool. Serve in bowls with a dollop of smatana or soured cream sprinkled with paprika. Garnish with dill if wished.

Beetroot borscht with soured cream

This makes a refreshing summer soup, served cold in a glass as is the custom in Israel.

I am passing on Jane Grigson's hint for keeping the colour bright. Boiling the beetroot turns it brown, so the Russian way is to make a separate beetroot juice to add to the finished stock to revive it.

4 large raw beetroots
2 tbsp raspberry vinegar
3 carrots, chopped
1 onion, chopped
4 sticks celery, chopped
salt
1 tbsp sugar
150 ml/¼ pint soured cream, to serve

1 First make the beetroot juice. Grate one beetroot into a bowl and just cover with boiling water. Add the vinegar and cook on HIGH for about 2½ minutes to bring back to the boil. Leave to infuse.
2 Put the carrots, onion and celery in another bowl and pour in enough boiling water to cover the vegetables. Cover and cook on HIGH for 10 minutes, then leave the vegetables soaking to strengthen the stock.
3 Grate the remaining 3 beetroots into a bowl, cover with water, then cook on HIGH for 8–10 minutes. Add the salt and sugar (less sugar if you don't like it sweet) and leave the stock to cool.
4 Strain the vegetable stock and the beetroot stock into a clear glass jug. Strain the beetroot juice and add this to improve the colour. Taste for seasoning and leave until cold. (There should be about 900 ml/1½ pints.) Pour into glasses or bowls and spoon in the soured cream.

Green marble soup

Jerusalem artichokes have a subtle flavour which is often hard to identify. Don't drown it with heavily seasoned stock cubes: simmer some vegetables in water with lamb or chicken bones, while you deal with the slightly tedious job of peeling the knobbly tubers.

½ lemon
700 g/1½ lb Jerusalem artichokes
1 tbsp oil
½ large Spanish onion, chopped
600 ml/1 pint lamb or chicken stock
salt and pepper
Watercress purée
1 bunch watercress
50 ml/2 fl oz lamb or chicken stock

1 Squeeze the lemon juice into a bowl of cold water and drop in the artichokes as you peel them.
2 Put the oil in a bowl and cook on HIGH for 40 seconds. Add the onion and cook on HIGH stirring once, for 1–2 minutes until softened.
3 Drain and slice the artichokes and add to the onions, stir, then cook on HIGH for 2 minutes. Add a little stock and cook for a further 4 minutes or until the vegetables are soft.
4 Purée in a food processor or blender with the rest of the stock and seasoning until smooth.
5 To make the purée, put the watercress and stock in a bowl and cook on HIGH for 1 minute, then purée separately.
6 Serve the soup in heated bowls and swirl in some of the watercress purée making a marbled effect with a fork.

Beetroot borscht with sour cream;
Green marble soup.

Pumpkin soup

I had never cooked pumpkin, believing it to be prettier than it tastes. On a chilly autumn day I was offered a bowl of delicious, steaming soup and was assured that it contained only cooked pumpkin and a soup cube. So here it is, quickly made and ready to serve in the most decorative container you can find.

1 pumpkin, about 2.25 kg/5 lb
2 vegetable or beef stock cubes
salt and pepper
freshly grated nutmeg

1 Stand the pumpkin on a firm surface with the stalk upwards. With a pencil, draw a scalloped pattern round the circumference, about a third of the way down. With a sharp knife, cut round the line, cutting into the flesh to form the lid. Loosen it carefully until the top comes off, then scoop out the seeds and any loose stringy flesh and discard.
2 Using a sharp curved knife or a melon baller, scoop out all the hard flesh, scraping it out carefully so as not to damage the shell.
3 Chop the flesh roughly and put half of it into a shallow dish. Sprinkle over 3 tbsp water, cover and cook on HIGH for 4 minutes, or until soft.
4 Stir 600 ml/1 pint boiling water into the stock cubes, then blend the cooked pumpkin with half the stock. Cook the remaining pumpkin the same way and blend with the rest to the stock. Taste for seasoning.
5 Heat the pumpkin shell on HIGH for 4 minutes, then keep it warm by filling it with boiling water. Replace the lid while you reheat the soup. Sprinkle with grated nutmeg. Pour away the water and fill the pumpkin shell with the hot soup.

Note: The French version of this soup can be sweet or savoury. The purée is thinned with milk or cream instead of stock and served with sugar, for children, or salt and pepper, for adults.

Vichyssoise of leek with watercress

The famous original of this summer soup included potatoes and a jugful of double cream. It's strange that the leeks – one of the dominant vegetables – are not in season in June or July, but the problem is solved if you freeze the leek purée earlier in the year. You can serve the soup hot or cold.

450 g/1 lb leeks
450 ml/¾ pint chicken or vegetable stock
1 bunch large spring onions, green and white
*   parts sliced separately*
1 bunch watercress
salt and black pepper
300 ml/½ pint milk
150 ml/¼ pint single cream
chopped chives

1 Discard the ends and tough outer leaves of the leeks. Chop the rest fairly thinly and wash thoroughly in several changes of cold water to remove any traces of grit. Drain.
2 Put in a dish with 150 ml/¼ pint stock, cover and cook on HIGH for 5–7 minutes, or until the leeks are tender.
3 Add the sliced white parts of the spring onions and cook for 3 minutes.
4 Chop the watercress, making sure there are no yellowing leaves or ends, and stir it into the leek and onion mixture. Continue cooking for 1½ minutes.
5 Season and purée the vegetables in a blender with the rest of the stock.
6 Pour in the milk and continue blending until the soup is smooth. Leave to cool, then stir in half the cream. Pour it into bowls and swirl in the rest of the cream and sprinkle with the chopped chives.

Note: Prepare the soup to the end of step 5 if you are freezing the purée. To serve hot, reheat gently with half cream and swirl in rest just before serving.

Mushroom and mozzarella toasts for soup

Guests are sometimes confused by the unfamiliar. What do you do with these, drop them in the soup or eat them instead of the rolls? Well, you can do either. The melted mozzarella topping stops the microwaved bread from being tooth-breakingly tough. Serve with Mushroom Velvet Soup (see p. 55) or Minestrone Soup (see p. 45).

150 g/5 oz mushrooms
25 g/1 oz butter
1 tbsp chopped fresh parsley
salt and pepper
8 thin slices rye bread
50 g/2 oz mozzarella cheese

1 If the mushrooms are very small leave them whole, otherwise slice them and put in a bowl with the butter, parsley and seasoning. Cook on HIGH for 1½ minutes.
2 Prepare the bread squares and the cheese. Cut off the crusts, leaving 8 neat squares. Slice the cheese thinly.
3 Arrange the bread squares on absorbent kitchen paper and lift on to a plate. Cook on HIGH for 50 seconds. Immediately spoon over the cooked, drained mushrooms, cover with the mozzarella cheese and cook for 1 minute. The cheese should be melted and soft. Serve the toasts immediately with bowls of hot soup.

Crispy noodles

Crispy noodles are normally deep-fried but if you have a combination cooker or even a microwave and a separate grill you can achieve a much quicker and less fattening result. You can nibble the crispy noodles with a drink or sprinkle a few into hot soup.

75 g/3 oz Chinese noodles
1 tsp sesame oil
1 tbsp soy sauce

1 Put the noodles in a shallow container and cover with boiling water. Cook on HIGH for 2 minutes, then leave to stand for 3 minutes. Drain well.
2 Preheat the grill and cover the grill pan with a sheet of foil. Toss the cooked noodles with the oil and soy sauce and spread them out over the foil.
3 Grill for about 3–4 minutes or until they are crispy and brown, turning them once to ensure they are evenly cooked.
4 Pile into a bowl and leave to get cold.

Garlic toast rounds

Keep these toast rounds warm and serve with hot soups or Soft Cheese and Vegetable Domes (see p. 99).

4 large slices granary bread
1 clove garlic, crushed
25 g/1 oz salted butter

1 Cut the bread with a round cutter into 16 small circles.
2 Mix the garlic with half the butter. Put it on a plate and cook on HIGH for 30 seconds. Mix in the rest of the butter.
3 Toast the bread well on one side and very lightly on the other. Spread this side with the garlic butter and brown under the grill for a few more seconds.

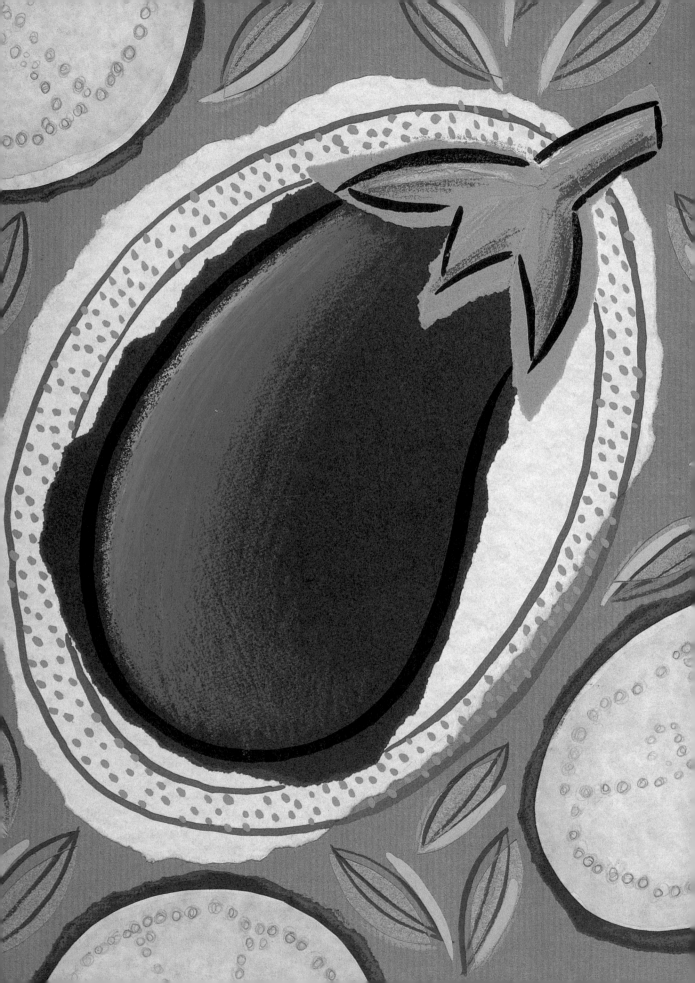

Main Courses

Fashions in food come and go, but it is another matter to change the habits of a lifetime. However, the way we eat today is slowly changing — for two reasons. The repeated warnings of the medical profession are now being taken seriously and we are being encouraged to abandon our traditional diet in favour of one which is low in fat and high in fibre. And there is a surge of interest in vegetarian food. In the light of these changes, the microwave and fresh vegetables are a winning combination. The food is very lightly cooked, so it is healthier. It looks pretty and appetising, so no-one is going to feel deprived when they see dishes like salmon trout in spinach envelopes or peppers with rice and cheese. I have intentionally changed the balance here of some well-known favourites, using smaller amounts of high-cholesterol foods and a large selection of vegetables. This does give rise to the question of how filling they are, so although most of them will serve four, it is always a good idea to choose one or two complementary dishes to go with them.

Vegetable and chicken risotto

When I was young and newly married, I served up what I thought was a passable risotto. My husband (yet to be impressed by my cooking) searched in vain for what he called recognizable pieces of anything and I have never been forgiven for the mean amount of chicken it contained! If you are one of those people who still feel the need of a large piece of meat as a main course, serve this risotto with a leg of chicken or steak on the side!

350 g/12 oz long-grain rice
1 tbsp olive oil
175 g/6 oz baby courgettes, trimmed
1 orange pepper, deseeded and sliced
350 g/12 oz cooked chicken, cut into large
  pieces
2 tbsp chicken fat or extra oil
1 large onion, finely chopped
1 large carrot, cut into sticks or slices
700 ml/24 fl oz chicken or beef stock
salt and pepper

1 Wash and thoroughly drain the rice.
2 Heat 1 tbsp oil in a dish on HIGH for 1 minute, add the courgettes and cook for 1 minute. Add the pepper slices and cook for another 2 minutes. Mix these vegetables with the chicken pieces and set aside.
3 Heat the chicken fat or oil in a dish on HIGH for 40 seconds, add the chopped onion and carrot slices and cook for 2 minutes. Make sure the rice is quite dry and stir it into the fat to coat all the grains. Cook for 1 minute on HIGH.
4 Stir in the stock, cover and cook on HIGH for 8 minutes. Mix in the chicken and vegetables and continue cooking for a further 2 minutes. Season well and leave to stand, covered, for another 10 minutes before serving.

Aubergines with cheese

As a child, I was always intrigued by the marvellous-sounding 'Mozzarella in carrozza'. These are nothing like those deep-fried ham and cheese sandwiches but the aubergines make a good vehicle for the melted mozzarella cheese. If you salt the cut halves, leave them to stand *and* microwave them before frying, you get rid of the bitter juices and reduce the amount of oil the aubergines absorb.

550 g/1¼ lb aubergines (2 large or 4 small)
salt and pepper
2–4 tbsp oil
½ onion, finely chopped
1 clove garlic, crushed
350 g/12 oz canned tomatoes, drained and
  chopped
½ tsp sugar
225 g/8 oz mozzarella cheese, thinly sliced

1 Cut the aubergines in half lengthwise and scoop out some of the flesh. Sprinkle shells and flesh with salt, then leave to drain for at least 30 minutes on absorbent kitchen paper.
2 Rinse in cold water, drain well and pat dry. Chop the flesh into cubes.
3 Cook the aubergine shells on HIGH for 3 minutes, then repeat with the cubes.
4 Heat half the oil in a frying pan on the stove and sauté the shells first, pressing them down slightly to make sure both sides are cooked. When the cut sides are brown, transfer to a serving dish.
5 Heat the rest of the oil and fry the onion and garlic until golden brown. Add the aubergine cubes and fry for a few more minutes. Add the tomatoes to the mixture, turning up the heat to reduce the amount of juice. Season with salt, pepper and sugar.
6 Spoon the filling into the shells and lay the sliced cheese over the top. Arrange the shells close together in a dish and cook on HIGH for about 3 minutes, or until the mozzarella has melted.

Peppers with green rice and cheese

Brown rice is a good standby for vegetarian meals since it takes about half the time to cook in the microwave. The 'green' in the title actually refers to finely chopped vegetables.

100 g/4 oz brown rice
900 ml/1½ pints boiling water
salt and pepper
4 red, orange or yellow peppers, halved and deseeded
2 tbsp olive oil
2 large spring onions, chopped
75 g/3 oz courgettes, chopped
75 g/3 oz French beans, chopped
100 g/4 oz grated Cheddar cheese
75 g/3 oz halved, toasted almonds

1 First cook the brown rice. Rinse it in cold water and then put it in a pot with the boiling water, cover and cook on HIGH for 15 minutes. Add salt, cook for a further 5 minutes, then leave to stand for 5 minutes.
2 Put the peppers in a dish and cook on HIGH for 3 minutes, then turn them over. Drizzle over 1 tbsp oil and cook for another 2–3 minutes, or until they are soft (the skin should peel off easily, but you don't have to remove it if it is stubborn). Arrange the peppers round the outside of a round dish.
3 Cook the onions and courgettes in the remaining oil on HIGH for 1½ minutes. Cook the beans with 1 tbsp water on HIGH for 1½ minutes. Mix the drained rice with the cooked vegetables and season to taste.
4 Fill the pepper halves with the rice mixture and spoon any extra into the centre of the dish. Sprinkle with the grated cheese and cook on HIGH for 2–4 minutes, or until the cheese is melted. Just before serving, scatter over the toasted almonds.

Mushroom and mozzarella pancakes

You should always reheat pancakes in the microwave uncovered, and if you prefer them crisp you should finish them off under a hot grill. For the best flavour, use freshly grated Parmesan cheese rather than pre-packed grated cheese.

8 pancakes (see p. 29)
25 g/1 oz butter
225 g/8 oz mushrooms, sliced
salt and black pepper
175 g/6 oz mozzarella cheese, thinly sliced
75 g/3 oz coarsely grated Parmesan cheese
300 ml/½ pint soured cream or smatana

1 Make the pancakes and lay them out flat.
2 Melt the butter in a dish on HIGH for 40 seconds. Add the mushrooms, turning them to coat with the melted butter and cook on HIGH for about 2 minutes. Season to taste.
3 Arrange the mushrooms and sliced mozzarella down the centre of the pancakes. Roll them up, tucking in the sides to make small parcels.
4 Arrange them in a dish in a single layer, sprinkle with the Parmesan cheese and cook on HIGH, uncovered, for 2½–4 minutes. The cheese inside will have melted and the pancakes should be very hot. Serve with chilled soured cream or smatana.

Note: This makes eight pancakes, so unless you are serving other dishes with it you may want to double the quantities and increase the cooking times.

Courgette and lamb moussakas

Serve these with rice or new potatoes.

6 large courgettes, about 450 g/1 lb
salt and pepper
1 tbsp oil
2 large onions, finely chopped
300 ml/½ pint chicken or light beef stock
1 quantity Tomato Sauce (see p. 21); omitting
 the onion
275 g/10 oz cooked lamb
1 tbsp chopped fresh mint or rosemary sprigs
2 egg whites

1 With a vegetable parer, cut the unpeeled courgettes into long thin slices, put in a dish, cover and cook on HIGH for 2 minutes. Season and leave to cool.
2 To make the onion soubise sauce, heat the oil in a dish on HIGH for 1 minute. Add the onions and cook on HIGH for 2 minutes. Add 6 tbsp stock and cook for a further 5 minutes or until the onion is soft. Purée the sauce until it is smooth and season well.
3 Make the tomato sauce as on p. 21.
4 Mince the lamb with the mint or rosemary and a few tablespoons of stock.
5 To assemble the moussakas, line five 75 ml/3 fl oz ramekins with some of the sliced courgettes, overlapping them slightly to make sure there are no gaps. Spoon in the lamb and add 1 tbsp of tomato sauce to each one. With a fork press the lamb and tomato mixture gently towards the edges, keeping it well inside the sliced courgettes.
6 Whisk the egg whites lightly and fold in half of the cooled onion purée. Pour this over the lamb and cover with the remaining courgette slices, tucking in any ends or trimming them with scissors.
7 Arrange the ramekins round the outside of a shallow container or directly on to the ceramic turntable. Cover lightly and cook on MEDIUM for 6 minutes. Leave to stand.

8 Pour the remaining sauces into small jugs and reheat on HIGH until they are hot.
9 Put a saucer over the top of each ramekin and pour off any juices. Turn them over on to large individual plates (they should slip out quite easily) and pour a little tomato sauce and onion sauce round the sides.

Beef salad

A continental salad made as it should be with fresh vegetables and good mayonnaise.

550 g/1¼ lb potatoes, diced
225 g/8 oz broad beans in the pods
225 g/8 oz fresh peas in the pods
75 g/3 oz French beans, topped and tailed
100 g/4 oz carrots, cut into dice or small rounds
salt and pepper
450 g/1 lb cooked roast beef or rare grilled steak,
 cooled and cut into dice
150 ml/¼ pint mayonnaise

1 Put the potatoes in a dish with boiling water coming halfway up and cook on HIGH for about 8 minutes, or until they are just cooked but not collapsing. Drain.
2 Meanwhile, shell the broad beans and peas. Put the broad beans in a dish with a few tablespoons of boiling water, cover and cook on HIGH for about 3 minutes. When they are cool enough, remove the tough outer shells.
3 Cook the peas in the same way for about 3 minutes, the French beans for 2–2½ minutes and the carrots for about 4 minutes. Season all the vegetables lightly after cooking and drain off any liquid. Leave to cool.
4 Mix the diced beef or steak with the cooked vegetables. Fold in the mayonnaise and pile on to a large platter or deep glass bowl.

Courgette and lamb moussaka; Crêpes provençales (see p. 72).

Crispy top pasta with aubergine sauce

In Italy, a pasta dish like this is served before the 'arrosto' or roast. If you serve large portions with a tossed green salad, it is a meal in itself.

2 quantities Tomato Sauce (see p. 36)
225 g/8 oz aubergines
salt and pepper
2 tbsp olive oil
1 onion, chopped
2 cloves garlic, crushed
100 g/4 oz mushrooms, sliced
500 g/1 lb 2 oz penne (quill pasta)
175 g/6 oz grated Cheddar or Parmesan cheese
100 g/4 oz fresh breadcrumbs

1 First make the tomato sauce, allowing extra time for simmering the double quantity – it will take 12–15 minutes altogether.
2 Salt, drain and cook the aubergine cubes (see p. 64).
3 Heat 1 tbsp oil in a frying pan and sauté the onion and garlic for a few minutes. Add the aubergine cubes and cook until they are beginning to brown.
4 Heat the rest of the oil in a bowl on HIGH for 1 minute, add the mushrooms and cook for 2 minutes.
5 Mix together the aubergines, mushrooms and the tomato sauce and season to taste.
6 Cook the pasta according to the packet instructions, drain well and toss with the sauce. Pour into a large greased dish. Mix together the cheese and breadcrumbs, sprinkle them over the top and cook on COMBINATION 7 (250C 40W) for about 10 minutes, or until the top is crispy and brown, or bake in a preheated oven at 190C (375F/ Gas 5) for 30 minutes.

Navarin of lamb

Tiny turnips or 'navets' are, according to Jane Grigson, 'a whole lifetime away from the yellow turnips of winter with their stringy waterlogged flesh'. The traditional navarin has more meat and a flour-based sauce; in this one the flavour of the vegetables dominates the small pieces of lamb in a light gravy.

450 ml/¾ pt Light Vegetable Stock (see p. 44)
salt and pepper
900 g/2 lb tender lamb (from the shoulder or leg) with the bones
8 small onions
625 g/1 lb 6 oz small new potatoes
450 g/1 lb small new carrots
12 tiny, mauve-tipped white turnips
1 clove garlic, chopped
large sprig fresh rosemary
1 tsp sugar

1 First make the stock (see p. 44), using lamb bones instead of chicken if preferred.
2 Dice the meat and sauté it in a non-stick frying pan over fairly high heat until the fat starts to run. Add the small onions and cook until both start to brown. Transfer to a microwave or combination casserole.
3 Put the potatoes in a dish with 150 ml/¼ pint boiling water and cook on HIGH for 5 minutes. Drain and set aside.
4 Pour the stock into the frying pan, bring it to the boil and deglaze the pan.
5 Mix the carrots and turnips with the meat and add the garlic, rosemary, sugar and seasoning. Pour over half the stock, cover and cook on HIGH for 15 minutes, then on LOW for 30 minutes. Add the potatoes and the rest of the stock and continue cooking on LOW for 7 minutes or until the lamb is tender. (Alternatively, add all the stock and cook on COMBINATION 4 (180C 190W) for about 1 hour, adding the potatoes near the end of the cooking time.)

Cheese omelette with soft buttered onions

One of my sons invited a friend to dinner. As I was about to carve the roast veal he announced 'I'm a vegetarian'. At that kind of notice, one could hardly do better than give him a glass of wine and reappear 5 minutes later with this.

1 tbsp oil
1 onion, finely chopped
50 g/2 oz butter
25 g/1 oz stick frozen whipping cream
50 g/2 oz Cheddar cheese
salt and pepper
3 eggs

1 Heat the oil in a bowl on HIGH for 40 seconds. Stir in the onion, coating it with the oil, and cook for 1 minute.
2 Add half the butter, cook on HIGH for 1 minute, stir the onion and cook for a further 3–4 minutes until it is soft.
3 Defrost the cream stick in a bowl for about 40 seconds. Stir in the buttered onions with the grated cheese and season with pepper and a little salt.
4 Meanwhile, in a separate bowl, whisk the eggs lightly with 1 tbsp water and season.
5 Melt 15g/½ oz butter in an omelette pan on the stove and when it begins to foam, pour in the eggs. Cook gently until the bottom of the omelette is just beginning to set. Lift the edges with a palette knife so that the uncooked egg pours out to the sides. Shake the pan, working quickly so that it is not too firm.
6 Spoon the cheese and onion mixture over the omelette and lift one side over the top. Spread the remaining butter over the surface and slide out on to a heated plate. Serve immediately.

Note: This makes enough for 1 omelette.

Chicken livers with chinese vegetables

This is a light main course, with interesting contrasts in texture.

350 g/12 oz chicken livers
2 tbsp oil
75 g/3 oz spring onions, chopped
75 g/3 oz mushrooms, sliced
100 g/4 oz mange-tout, topped and tailed
100 g/4 oz Chinese leaves, shredded
100 g/4 oz beansprouts
salt and pepper
2–4 tbsp soy sauce
boiled rice or noodles, to serve

1 Wash and dry the livers well and cut into small pieces.
2 Heat half the oil in a dish on HIGH for 1 minute and cook the livers for about 3 minutes, stirring halfway through. If you like the livers pink test after a few minutes – if not, continue until they seem cooked. Transfer the livers to a heated dish and keep warm.
3 Heat the rest of the oil in a dish on HIGH for 1 minute. Add the onions and mushrooms, stir and cook on HIGH for 2 minutes.
4 Stir in the mange-tout with the Chinese leaves and beansprouts and continue cooking for 2 minutes. Season very lightly, then stir in half the soy sauce.
5 Arrange the vegetables on hot plates, pile the livers on top and serve immediately, drizzled with the rest of the soy sauce. Serve with noodles or rice.

Tomatoes with sole and two sauces

12 large, firm tomatoes
2 lemon soles, filleted and skinned, about 1.4
  kg/3 lb on bone
150 ml/¼ pint dry white wine
25 g/1 oz butter
1 tbsp plain flour
50 ml/2 fl oz cream or 2 frozen sticks, thawed
2 tsp tomato purée
salt and pepper
pinch sugar

1 Peel the tomatoes as on p.18. Cut off the tops and reserve, then scoop out the insides of the tomatoes with a curved sharp knife (being careful not to pierce the bases). Reserve the tomato pulp and juice. Season the tomatoes lightly, then turn upside down and leave to drain.
2 Cut the fish fillets lengthwise into 8 pieces, then crosswise to make 16. Pour over the wine, sprinkle with salt and pepper and roll them up. Arrange in a dish in a single layer fairly close together, cover and cook on HIGH for 2½ minutes, turning them over once during this time. Strain off the cooking juice and reserve.
3 To make the wine sauce, melt the butter slightly in a jug, then stir in the flour. Pour on the reserved cooking juices and cook on HIGH, stirring once or twice for about 1 minute, or until the sauce is thick and smooth. Stir in the cream.
4 To make the tomato sauce, add the tomato purée and seasoning to the tomato pulp and juice in a separate jug or bowl. Cover and cook on HIGH for about 4 minutes, then press the sauce through a strainer.
5 To assemble the dish, first dry the tomatoes well. Mash 4 of the rolled up fish pieces and spoon some of this into the base of each tomato. Cover with a spoonful of the wine sauce, then arrange a rolled fillet in each one.

Replace the tomato tops and arrange the stuffed tomatoes in a round dish.
6 Cook the tomatoes on HIGH for 3–4½ minutes, until hot. Cover them and keep warm while you reheat the 2 jugs of sauce.
7 Serve on warmed plates with a spoonful of each sauce on the side.

Salmon trout in spinach envelopes

1.4 kg/3 lb salmon trout, skinned and filleted
25 g/1 oz butter
1 tbsp chopped fresh dill
grated rind of 1 lemon
salt and pepper
225–450 g/8 oz–1 lb fresh spinach (large
  leaves)

1 Trim the salmon trout into eight 7.5 cm/3 in squares and remove all the bones.
2 Mix the butter with the dill, lemon rind, salt and pepper.
3 Wash the spinach well, drain it and then choose 8 of the best shaped large leaves. Remove the stalks and cook on HIGH for 30 seconds to soften them.
4 Arrange the spinach on a layer of absorbent kitchen paper, press over another layer to absorb any moisture and then season the leaves lightly.
5 Place a salmon trout square on each leaf and spread over some of the butter mixture. Fold over the spinach to make a neat envelope, then arrange them with the joins downwards in a shallow round dish.
6 Cover and cook on HIGH for 4 minutes. If the butter oozes out, brush it over the top of the spinach before serving.

Salmon trout in spinach envelopes; Tomatoes with sole and two sauces.

Crêpes provençales

The ratatouille filling for these pancakes can be speeded up with the microwave, though you still need to do some cooking in a frying pan on the top of the stove to get the right flavour.

225 g/8 oz aubergines
salt and pepper
4 tbsp oil
175 g/6 oz yellow or orange peppers, deseeded and cut into strips
225 g/8 oz courgettes, sliced
1 onion, chopped
1 clove garlic, crushed
3 tomatoes, skinned (see p. 20) and chopped
8 pancakes (see p. 29)
2–3 tbsp coarsely grated Parmesan cheese

1 Cut the aubergines into small dice, sprinkle with plenty of salt and leave to drain on a wire rack over absorbent kitchen paper for about 20 minutes.
2 Heat ½ tbsp oil in a dish on HIGH for 40 seconds, stir in the peppers and cook for 2 minutes. Stir and cook for another 2 minutes. In a separate dish, heat 1 tbsp oil for 40 seconds, add the courgettes and cook for 3 minutes, stirring halfway through.
3 Rinse and drain the aubergines and cook on HIGH for 3 minutes.
4 In a frying pan, heat half the remaining oil and sauté the onion and garlic until the onion starts to soften. Add the aubergine cubes with the rest of the oil and continue frying until the vegetables are brown. Stir in the chopped tomatoes, season with salt and pepper and cook for about 3 minutes. Add the peppers and courgettes and taste for seasoning.
5 Lay out the pancakes and divide the filling equally between them. Fold or roll them up and arrange them fairly close together in a round or oval dish. Sprinkle with Parmesan cheese and cook, uncovered, on HIGH for about 5 minutes or until the filling it hot.

Mange-tout salad with avocados and smoked turkey

For the vegetables to outshine the meat in a dish, they have to be especially good. A useful test is to see if they taste good raw. Try to find small mange-tout because the larger ones can be stringy and tough.

2 carrots, cut into long sticks
100 g/4 oz runner beans, sliced diagonally
225 g/8 oz mange-tout, topped and tailed
3 tbsp soy sauce
225 g/8 oz smoked turkey, chicken or beef, sliced
2 ripe avocados
2 tbsp lemon juice
3 tbsp oil
1 tbsp wine vinegar
salt and black pepper

1 Put the carrots and beans in a dish with 4 tbsp water, cover and cook on HIGH for 3–5 minutes, depending on how crisp you like them. Add the mange-tout and cook for 1 minute. Drain, then sprinkle over the soy sauce and toss the vegetables to coat them evenly.
2 Leave to cool slightly, then mix the meat with the cooked vegetables.
3 Peel and halve the avocados and pour over the lemon juice. Whisk together the oil and vinegar, season lightly and spoon a little of this dressing over the drained avocados.
4 Arrange the meat and vegetables on one side of a platter. Cut the avocado in slices and arrange these, with the dressing, down the other side. Serve immediately.

Spinach and fish terrine

The difficult part of cooking a rectangular-shaped terrine in the microwave is to get the centre cooked. However, preparing the layers is easy and the finished result looks a lot more complicated than it really is.

275 g/10 oz salmon or salmon trout fillet
120 ml/4 fl oz cream
salt and pepper
2 egg whites
225 g/8 oz lemon sole or haddock fillet
25 ml/1 fl oz fish stock or 15 g/½ oz butter
450 g/1 lb fresh spinach
1 egg yolk
50 g/2 oz ricotta cheese
Red or Yellow Pepper Coulis (see p. 37), to
*   serve*

1 First prepare the layers. For the salmon layer, process the salmon or trout with half the cream and seasoning in a food processor or blender. Gradually add 1 egg white until the mixture is very smooth. Chill in fridge.
2 Put the white fish in a dish with the stock or butter, cover and cook on HIGH for 2 minutes, or until it flakes easily. Drain well, then process it with the rest of the cream and the other egg white. Taste for seasoning – it should not be too bland.
3 Wash and dry the spinach. Put in a dish and cook on HIGH for 2–3 minutes, or until it is soft. Drain and season well, then process it with the egg yolk and ricotta until the mixture is fairly smooth.
4 Put half the spinach mixture in the base of a 600 ml/1 pint glass or plastic terrine mould. Cover with half the salmon mixture, then spread all the white fish over the top. Cover with the rest of the salmon and finish with the remaining spinach. Cover and cook on MEDIUM for 5–6 minutes. The terrine should be just firm to the touch and not tacky on top and the sides should come away easily if you slide a knife round the edges.
5 Carefully pour off any liquid, then leave to cool in the mould. When the terrine is cold, run a knife round the edges, place a long plate over the top and carefully turn it over. Leave to chill in the refrigerator. Mop up any extra juices with absorbent kitchen paper, then slice the terrine into 1 cm/½ in slices. Serve with Red or Yellow Pepper Coulis, or both.

Courgette and tomato pasta bake

This reheats very well in the microwave so all the work can be done in advance.

1 quantity Béchamel Sauce (see p. 32)
1 quantity Tomato Sauce (see p. 36)
2 tomatoes
2 tbsp olive oil
450 g/1 lb courgettes, sliced
500 g/1 lb 2 oz tagliatelle
15 g/½ oz butter
salt and pepper

1 First prepare the 2 sauces.
2 Peel the tomatoes (see p. 20) and chop them into small pieces, discarding the seeds.
3 Heat the oil in a dish on HIGH for 1 minute, add the courgettes and cook on HIGH for 2 minutes. Using a slotted spoon, transfer them to a plate, then cook the tomato pieces in the same oil on HIGH for 1 minute.
4 Cook the tagliatelle according to the packet instructions and drain it well.
5 Butter a large round gratin dish. Strain the tomato sauce and mix it with the béchamel, making sure it is well seasoned. Stir in the tomato pieces and the pasta and pour into the dish. Arrange the rings of courgette all over the top, pressing some into the pasta if there are too many for one layer.
6 To serve immediately, put the dish under a preheated grill until the vegetables are just turning brown.
7 To reheat, cook on HIGH until the centre is hot and then grill as above, or cook on COMBINATION 7 (250C 40W) for 20 minutes.

Side Dishes

The vegetables you serve on the side should
be as carefully chosen as any main dish.
They should be complementary but never
overwhelming, so it isn't a good idea to
introduce too many contrasting flavours.
Even in the best restaurants, a waiter will often
give you plenty of time to choose your favourite
dish and then hurriedly offer to bring you 'just a
selection of vegetables'. It's very unlikely that sauté
potatoes, ratatouille and creamed spinach will go
equally well with duck, sole or steak.
The microwave is excellent for cooking vegetables
as a side dish. If you like the idea of entertaining with
the restaurant touch and giving each guest a separate
plate of vegetables, you can lightly pre-cook them one
at a time, and then arrange them in well-chosen com-
binations ready to reheat in minutes as you bring on the
main course. For family meals, dishes that used to take
hours can now be served up in 30 minutes

Courgette and carrot sticks

Expensive restaurants offer a *bouquetière de légumes,* which is another way of describing 'vegetables of the day'. Serving them at home, freshly cooked, needs some organization. My suggestion is to have ready four plates of boiled new potatoes with mint and keep them warm for the few minutes it takes to microwave these sticks.

225 g/8 oz carrots
275 g/10 oz courgettes
6 tbsp vegetable or chicken stock
salt and pepper
juice of 1 lemon
To serve
cooked new potatoes sprinkled with chopped
   fresh mint
butter

1 Cut the carrots and courgettes into long sticks. (The even shapes help them to cook quickly.)
2 Put the carrot sticks in a dish with 3 tbsp stock, cover and cook on HIGH for 3 minutes. Drain and season, then keep covered with a warm plate.
3 Cook the courgette sticks with the same amount of stock for 2 minutes and keep warm in the same way.
4 Arrange the new potatoes on 4 plates. Squeeze the lemon juice over the vegetable sticks and divide them evenly between the plates. Dot with butter and serve immediately.

Spring vegetables with mint butter

One of the problems of microwaving is keeping different dishes warm. You can solve this by cooking several vegetables separately in advance, arranging them on a platter and reheating them so that they will be piping hot when you bring them to the table. If you prefer the vegetables slightly crisp, remember to undercook them to allow for the extra cooking later.

225 g/8 oz asparagus tips
350 g/12 oz salsify
225 g/8 oz flat Spanish beans
350 g/12 oz courgettes
salt and pepper
50 g/2 oz butter
1 tsp lemon juice
1 tbsp chopped fresh mint

1 First prepare all the vegetables. Cut the stalks off the asparagus and reserve them for soup or stock. Peel the salsify and drop it into acidulated water (see p. 17). Cut the beans into 5 cm/2 in lengths and the courgettes into sticks.
2 Put the vegetables in separate dishes with 2–3 tablespoons water, cover and cook on HIGH: asparagus, for 5 minutes, salsify for 5–7 minutes, beans for 5 minutes and courgettes for 4 minutes. Season lightly and drain.
3 Arrange the cooked vegetables on a round dish.
4 Mix the butter with the lemon juice and chopped mint and divide it into 4 portions. When ready to serve, dot the butter over the vegetables, cover and reheat for a few minutes. The butter should be melted and the vegetables hot. Serve immediately.

Vegetable kebabs

The trouble with kebabs is that you are combining foods that may look pretty but require different cooking times. Vegetables are no exception, so microwaving some of them first is a good idea.

12 small onions
4 carrots
4 courgettes
2 peppers
12 button mushrooms
12 cherry tomatoes
1 tbsp oil
Baste
2 tbsp soy sauce
1 tsp brown sugar
1 tbsp oil

1 To make the baste, put the soy sauce and sugar in a bowl and cook on HIGH for about 30 seconds. Stir in the oil and leave to cool.
2 Prepare all the vegetables. Wash and peel the onions and carrots, trim the courgettes and peppers and wipe the tomatoes and mushrooms. Cut the carrots and courgettes into rings of about 0.5 cm (¼ in) and the peppers into even-sized pieces.
3 Put the carrots and onions in a dish, sprinkle with a few tablespoons of water, cover and cook on HIGH for about 4 minutes, or until tender.
4 Put the oil in a separate dish and cook on HIGH for 1 minute. Add the courgettes and peppers and cook for 2 minutes. Prick the mushrooms and tomatoes to prevent them bursting (there is no need to pre-cook them).
5 Thread all the vegetables except the tomatoes and mushrooms on to wooden skewers. Brush all the vegetables with the baste.
6 Cook the kebabs on HIGH for a few minutes until very hot. Add the tomatoes and mushrooms, cooking for another minute and serve immediately.

Leeks and runner beans with lemon sauce

A late summer dish which would go well with grilled or barbecued fish.

450 g/1 lb leeks
450 ml/¾ pint Light Vegetable Stock (see p. 44)
450 g/1 lb runner beans
grated rind and juice of 1 lemon
40 g/1½ oz butter
25 g/1 oz flour
salt and pepper

1 Slice the leeks across into rounds, wash them well, then drain off the excess water. Put in a dish with 6 tablespoons of the stock, cover and cook on HIGH for 6 minutes.
2 Remove the stringy sides of the beans with a sharp knife and slice them diagonally. Put them in a separate dish, sprinkle over 6 tablespoons of stock, cover and cook on HIGH for 5 minutes.
3 Season both vegetables and arrange them on individual dishes or on a large platter. Sprinkle over the lemon rind and keep covered while making the sauce.
4 Mix half the butter with the flour in a bowl and gradually add the remaining stock, stirring well. Cook on HIGH, stirring again, until the sauce thickens, 1–2 minutes. Pour in lemon juice to taste and stir in the rest of the butter. Season lightly.
5 Spoon the hot sauce over the vegetables and serve immediately.

Green salad with hot buttered mushrooms

The idea for this salad came from the inspired book *Vegetarian Epicure* by Anna Thomas. The leaves and herbs can be prepared in advance but the dressing and mushrooms should be added at the very last minute. There is a big difference between 'salade tiède' and soggy, wilted lettuce.

1 large hearty cos lettuce
1 small bunch fresh chives
few parsley sprigs
12 mint leaves
Dressing
3 tbsp olive oil
1 tbsp raspberry vinegar
salt and black pepper
Topping
40 g/1½ oz salted butter
175 g/6 oz small button mushrooms

1 Discard the tough outer leaves of the lettuce and wash and dry the heart, separating the leaves rather than cutting them. Put the leaves into a large bowl.
2 Freshen the herbs in ice cold water and dry well. Divide them into 4 piles.
3 When ready to serve the salad, make the dressing. Whisk together the oil and vinegar, season to taste then pour over the lettuce. Toss well to coat all the leaves. Arrange the tossed salad on 4 plates with the herbs sprinkled lightly over the top.
4 Melt the butter for the topping in a bowl on HIGH for 1 minute. Stir in the mushrooms and cook for 2 minutes, until the juices run. Sprinkle with black pepper and immediately spoon them over the salads.

Green salad with hot buttered mushrooms;
Spring vegetables with mint butter (see p. 76).

Fanned roast potatoes

If you have a family who will eat roast potatoes with anything (cold beef, sausages, even kippers!) here's something that can be cooking while you set the table and wait for them all to appear.

900 g/2 lb potatoes
1–2 tbsp oil
salt and pepper

1 Peel the potatoes and if they are large cut them into even sizes. Slice them downwards to within 0.5 cm/¼ in of the bottom, making thin slices that will fan out as they cook.
2 Arrange the slices in a glass baking dish. Sprinkle over a little boiling water, cover and cook on HIGH for 5 minutes.
3 Brush over the oil and cook on COMBINATION 8 (250C 275W) for about 25–30 minutes. Season lightly and serve hot.

Note: If you don't have a combination cooker, cook as normal roast potatoes, but they will take twice as long.

Stir-fried vegetables with pasta bows

This colourful, delicious side dish will go with everything – a quick and healthy alternative to chips!

1 tbsp oil
2 large carrots, thinly sliced diagonally
2 spring onions, chopped
2 courgettes, thinly sliced diagonally
75 g/3 oz button mushrooms, sliced
1 tbsp soy sauce
salt and pepper
225 g/8 oz cooked pasta bows (see note below)

1 Put the oil in a dish and cook on HIGH for 1 minute to heat. Add the carrots and onions and cook on HIGH for 2 minutes. Add the courgettes and cook for 1 minute and then add the mushrooms and cook for a further 1 minute. Stir in half the soy sauce and taste for seasoning.
2 Cook the pasta bows in a bowl on HIGH for 1 minute to reheat. Stir in the vegetables with the rest of the soy sauce and cook for 1 minute. Serve immediately on warmed plates.

Note: Left-over cooked pasta keeps well in the refrigerator for a few days and can be speedily revived in a dish like this. For 225 g/8 oz cooked pasta, you will need about 100 g/4 oz raw pasta.
   This makes enough for 4 side dishes but could also serve one hungry teenager alone. To increase the quantities, add more oil and cook the vegetables for longer.

Braised celery

Large celery heads are sometimes full of earth and are not suitable for this recipe as you would need to scrub each stalk carefully. Microwaving the small heads first cuts down the cooking time, but you need to continue with a combination cooker or normal oven to achieve the traditional dark colour. If you prefer not to use beef stock, you could use tomato juice and light vegetable stock instead.

950 g/2 lb 2 oz celery heads (4 or 5)
300 ml/½ pint strong beef stock or half and half
vegetable stock and tomato juice
salt and pepper

1 Cut the ends off the celery, split the heads in half horizontally and wash them well.
2 Arrange them in a single layer in an ovenproof glass dish and pour over half the stock or stock and tomato juice. Cover and cook on HIGH for 5 minutes.
3 Season well, pour in the rest of the liquid and cook on COMBINATION 4 (180C 190W) for 20 minutes. Alternatively, bake, covered, in a preheated oven 190C (375F/Gas 5) for about 40 minutes, or continue microwaving for 10 minutes on HIGH. In each case, turn the heads over halfway through the cooking time and baste with the stock.
4 Use a pointed knife to see if the celery heads are tender and serve hot, with the juices spooned over the top.

Candied sweet potatoes

When I was young, slim and always hungry I worked for a while in the U.S.A. and was introduced to a wonderful concoction of sweet, spiced potatoes with maple syrup. Recently I started thinking about speeding it up with a microwave and doing without some of the waist-thickening ingredients. Here is the result.

875 g/1¾ lb sweet potatoes
15–25 g/½–1 oz butter
1 tbsp golden or maple syrup
2 tsp lemon juice
salt and pepper

1 Peel the sweet potatoes and cut them into fairly thick slices. Cook in a gratin dish on HIGH for 5 minutes.
2 Put the butter and syrup in a jug and cook on HIGH for 40 seconds to melt, then pour in the lemon juice.
3 Season the potato slices and brush with the syrup. Cook on COMBINATION 8 (250C 275W) for about 25 minutes or until the potatoes are soft and the tops are browned. Alternatively bake in a preheated oven at 190C (375F/Gas 5) for about 40 minutes.

Parsnip timbales with watercress sauce

These faintly sweet timbales go surprisingly well with roasted meat or grilled fish. The green stripe in the centre is made with frozen beans or peas and the watercress in the sauce adds a peppery 'bite'.

225 g/8 oz parsnips, peeled and chopped
about 300 ml/½ pint strong vegetable stock
65 ml/2½ fl oz whipping cream
salt and pepper
1 egg white
275 g/10 oz frozen broad beans or peas
100 g/4 oz watercress

1 Put the parsnips in a dish with 4 tbsp stock, cover and cook on HIGH for 4–5 minutes or until they are soft.
2 Process the parsnips with 75 ml/3 fl oz stock in a blender or food processor to a thick purée. Add the cream and continue processing. Taste for seasoning, then add the egg white, processing once more to make a smooth mixture.
3 Cook the beans or peas with no extra liquid on HIGH for about 3–4 minutes. Purée in the blender with enough stock to moisten (about 25 ml/1 fl oz), then press through a sieve to remove the skins.
4 Pour half the parsnip purée into six 50 ml/2 fl oz ramekins. Using half the bean purée, spoon over a thin layer, pushing it gently towards the sides. Reserve the rest of the bean purée for the sauce. Cover the green purée with the remaining parsnip mixture, levelling the tops with a knife.
5 Arrange the ramekins round the edge of a shallow dish and cook, covered, on MEDIUM for 4–5 minutes, or until the mixture comes slightly away from the edges of the ramekins. Leave to stand.
6 Wash and dry the watercress and reserve a little for garnishing. Remove the stalks from the rest, then cook on HIGH for 1 minute.

Spoon into the blender with the remaining bean purée and 50 ml/2 fl oz stock, purée, then press through a sieve.
7 Run a knife round the edges of the timbales, turn them out on to small plates and surround with some of the watercress sauce. Garnish with the reserved watercress sprigs. Serve the rest of the sauce separately.

Salsify and courgette curls

Salsify is delicately flavoured, and there are two types: white salsify and black-skinned scorzonera. Salsify is sometimes called vegetable oyster or oyster plant.

½ lemon
350 g/12 oz salsify
350 g/12 oz courgettes
salt and pepper
lemon vinaigrette, to serve

1 Squeeze the lemon juice into a bowl of cold water and add the lemon.
2 Peel the salsify, cut into even lengths and put them immediately into the acidulated water to stop them discolouring.
3 With a vegetable peeler, cut the courgettes into very thin strips, leaving a dark line of skin at each side. Roll up the strips and secure them 2 at a time on wooden cocktail sticks, leaving a space between them.
4 Drain the salsify, put in a dish with 3 tbsp fresh water, cover and cook on HIGH for 5–7 minutes. Sprinkle with salt and pepper and leave to cool.
5 Put the courgette curls in a separate dish with no added water, cover and cook on HIGH for 1½–2 minutes; season as they cool.
6 Arrange the salsify like the spokes of a wheel on a flat dish. Remove the cocktail sticks and dot the courgettes around the spokes. Serve with lemon vinaigrette.

Salsify and courgette curls; Parsnip timbales with watercress sauce.

Potato gratin

It is often thought that a 'gratin' must contain cheese, but the name comes from the oval earthenware dish in which the vegetables are cooked. If you use a combination cooker the potatoes will brown in half the normal time.

15 g/½ oz butter
700 g/1½ lb potatoes
5 spring onions, chopped
salt and pepper
150–225 ml/5–8 fl oz cream

1 Spread the butter round the inside of a 25 cm/10 in gratin dish. Slice the potatoes fairly thinly, rinse them quickly, then arrange the slices in the dish. Cook on HIGH for 3 minutes.
2 Sprinkle the spring onions over the potatoes, season with salt and pepper and pour over 150 ml/¼ pint cream (you will need more if you are going to bake the gratin conventionally).
3 Cook, uncovered, on COMBINATION 5 (230C 220W) for 20–25 minutes.

Alternatively cook in a preheated oven at 220C (400F/Gas 6) for 30–40 minutes, making sure that the potatoes do not dry out completely. They should be soft inside and lightly browned on top.

Spanish rice with tomatoes

Oriental fried rice has separate grains as it is boiled first and then tossed in oil. Portuguese or Spanish rice is fried first, with the liquid added later. As it absorbs twice its volume of water, it becomes slightly sticky. Using the microwave doesn't save much time, but you can safely leave it cooking without worrying that you'll come back to a burnt saucepan.

225 g/8 oz long-grain rice
2 tbsp oil
100 g/4 oz onions, chopped
1 clove garlic, crushed
450 ml/¾ pint hot beef stock or water
3 tsp tomato purée
salt and pepper
2 tomatoes, quartered and peeled

1 Cover the rice with cold water, stir and leave soaking for a few minutes to release the starch. Drain and rinse well, then dry with absorbent kitchen paper.
2 Put the oil in a dish and cook on HIGH for 2 minutes. Add the onion and cook for 3 minutes. Stir in the garlic and cook for 2 minutes.
3 Add the rice, cook for 30 seconds on HIGH, then pour in the hot stock or water, with the tomato purée and seasoning (do not add much salt if you have used a cube to make stock). Stir well and cook on HIGH, covered, for 8 minutes. Stir in the quartered tomatoes and continue cooking for about 1½ minutes, or until the liquid is absorbed. Leave to stand for about 5 minutes before serving.

Indian spiced vegetables

Some Indian friends once offered to teach my son how to make vegetable curry. Their ten-year-old son went with mine to buy the spices and came back with eight different jars – all in the jumbo economy size. The Indian boy didn't realize that although his large family used spices every day, we were new to this and that by the time we'd mastered it, the spices would all be stale!

2 tbsp oil
½ tsp each cumin and coriander seed
2 large onions, finely chopped
2 cloves garlic, crushed
75 g/3 oz green pepper, cut into small pieces
100 g/4 oz carrots, cut into small pieces
100 g/4 oz runner beans, cut into small pieces
½ tsp turmeric powder
½ tsp ground cumin
¼ tsp chilli powder (or more for hot curry)
1 tbsp tomato purée
1 tbsp lemon juice
salt
50 g/2 oz broccoli, divided into small florets
50 g/2 oz cauliflower, divided into small florets
75 g/3 oz mushrooms, sliced
75 g/3 oz natural yogurt

1 Heat half the oil in a frying pan and add the cumin and coriander seeds. Almost immediately add the onions and garlic and stir until the onions start to turn transparent. Add the rest of the oil and fry the pepper, carrots and beans. Stir in the turmeric, ground cumin and chilli powder and then add the tomato purée, lemon juice and salt.
2 Transfer the vegetables to a dish, cover and cook on HIGH for 3–5 minutes, or until tender. Add the broccoli, cauliflower and mushrooms with 150 ml/¼ pint water and cook on HIGH for 4 minutes until the vegetables are soft but not mushy. Check the seasoning. Add the yogurt and reheat gently.
3 Serve the curried vegetables with plain boiled rice and extra yogurt or raita.

Broccoli and cauliflower with cheese sauce

Mark Twain said that 'Cauliflower is nothing but cabbage with a college education'. Even so, many people find it insipid and dull. Cauliflower cheese used to involve long boiling, but this method keeps the crunch and looks pretty, too.

450 g/1 lb broccoli
400 g/14 oz cauliflower
7 tbsp vegetable stock
salt and pepper
300 ml/½ pint Cheese Sauce (see p. 32)
50 g/2 oz toasted flaked almonds

1 Separate the broccoli into long florets and the cauliflower into short ones (keep the stalks for soup).
2 Arrange the broccoli as on p. 16, sprinkle with half the stock and cook, covered, on HIGH for 4 minutes. Season lightly.
3 Cook the cauliflower florets in a separate dish with the rest of the stock for about 4 minutes. Sprinkle with salt.
4 Strain the stock into the cheese sauce and pour the sauce over the base of a large round dish. Arrange the broccoli round the edge with the stalks facing inwards. Re-form the cauliflower florets into a 'head' in the centre. Serve the toasted almonds separately or the sauce will make them go soft.

Spinach parcels with peas

The restaurant trick for fresh vegetables is to prepare and blanch them earlier, then cook them again briefly just before serving. If you don't have a chef in the kitchen, just fill the spinach leaves in advance and while someone else is carving the joint, quickly cook them in the microwave.

450 g/1 lb large, fresh spinach leaves
225 g/8 oz frozen petit pois
salt and pepper

1 Wash the spinach leaves, removing all the stems and choose 16 fairly large even-sized ones. Drain then put in a dish and cook on HIGH, covered, for 1 minute. Dry the leaves carefully with absorbent kitchen paper and lay them out with the under-side upwards.
2 Put the peas in a dish and cook on HIGH for 1 minute to get rid of any ice. Drain well.
3 Spoon the peas on to the spinach leaves, season with salt and pepper and wrap each one carefully, tucking in the sides and rolling them over.
4 Arrange the parcels fairly close together in a round dish, leaving a space in the centre, and cook on HIGH for 2 minutes. Serve the spinach parcels immediately.

Spinach parcels with peas; Indian spiced vegetables (see p. 85); Stir-fried vegetables with pasta bows (see p. 80).

Stir-fried beansprouts

This is a good side dish for barbecued spare ribs or duck as it is crisp and light. A slightly drier version (with less soy sauce) makes an ideal stuffing for Chinese pancakes.

2 tbsp oil
50 g/2 oz orange or green peppers, cut into thin
 rings
2 large spring onions, sliced
100 g/4 oz mushrooms, sliced
350 g/12 oz beansprouts
2 tbsp soy sauce
salt and pepper

1 Heat half the oil in a dish on HIGH for 1 minute. Add the pepper slices and cook on HIGH for 2 minutes. Stir in the spring onions and mushrooms and cook for 1 minute. Stir the mixture again, add the rest of the oil and fold in the beansprouts. Cook for 1 minute.
2 Pour in the soy sauce, sprinkle with pepper and taste for seasoning, adding a little salt if necessary. Cook on HIGH for a further 30 seconds and serve immediately.

Note: As this dish is so quick to make it should never be made in advance. The beansprouts will lose their crispness if they are reheated.

Buttered corn cobs

This is the only vegetable you should buy if the outside looks withered! The golden hair inside the cobs turns black at the tips even when the corn is still fresh and plump inside. It should ideally be eaten within hours of being cut and the length of time it takes to cook depends mainly on how fresh it is. It is impossible to be precise and the only way to tell if it is done is to pull out a few kernels to taste. The normal method is to cook the cobs in plenty of boiling water. The microwave version is ideal if you just want to cook one or two.

2 corn cobs
softened butter for serving
salt and pepper

1 Trim off the corn stalks and a few of the outer leaves. Chop off the tops and the dark hairs.
2 Put the corn in a shallow dish. Open out the leaves and sprinkle each cob with a few tablespoons of boiling water. Cover and cook on HIGH for 3–4 minutes. Test to see if they are done by loosening 1 or 2 kernels with a fork – if they seem soft and come away easily the corn is cooked.
3 Carefully remove the leaves and the hairs, drain off any liquid and put each cob on to a heated plate. Spread over softened butter and sprinkle with salt and pepper.

Note: Add the salt at the end, even if you boil the corn in the normal way, otherwise it will make the kernels tough.

Kohlrabi au gratin

These purple or pale green root vegetables are best if they are small – no larger than a peach. Some people grate them over salads, others turn them into soup. Butter and cheese definitely improve them, but it is worth trying this small amount to see if you like the flavour.

4 small kohlrabi, peeled and cut into thin slices
salt and pepper
15 g/½ oz butter
25 g/1 oz cheese, grated

1 Arrange the kohlrabi slices in a single layer in a shallow dish. Pour in enough boiling water to come halfway up the sides of the dish, cover and cook on HIGH for 6 minutes, or until they are tender. Drain off the water and season very well.
2 Butter an ovenproof glass dish and arrange the kohlrabi in overlapping slices. Sprinkle with the cheese.
3 Cook on HIGH for a further 2–3 minutes to melt the cheese. Alternatively put under a hot grill to brown the top.

Note: This makes enough for about 3–4 people.

Spinach with oil and garlic

My Italian friends think that all English vegetables are hopelessly bland. At their suggestion I am including the 'only way' to cook them – it works for spring greens and Brussels sprouts too. Preparing fresh spinach is a tedious job and a huge mound disappears to almost nothing when it is cooked. But before you reach for the frozen variety, which won't be as good, try instead to find a nice piece of music to listen to while you prepare the spinach. This recipe should only take as long as the first movement of one of the Brandenberg concertos!

900 g/2 lb fresh spinach
salt and black pepper
2–3 cloves garlic, crushed
3–5 tbsp extra virgin olive oil
lemon wedges, to serve

1 Wash the spinach very well and remove all the stems and veins. The best way to do this is to fold the leaf in half and pull the stem out. Rinse and drain well.
2 Put half the spinach in a large dish, cover and cook on HIGH for 2–3 minutes, or until it is soft. Repeat with the remaining spinach.
3 Season with salt and pepper and drain again, extremely well. It must be quite dry. (You can prepare the dish in advance up to this stage and it even improves if you leave it to cool so that you can squeeze out all the moisture.) Chop the spinach roughly.
4 Put the garlic and oil in a large dish and cook on HIGH for 1 minute. Immediately toss in the spinach, turning it over until it is well coated with the garlicky oil. Reheat again if it is cold and serve with wedges of lemon.

Cool
Vegetable Platters

Cold food has unfortunate connotations – it's either left over from a previous hot meal, or it is just dreary and dull. Room service menus in hotels often feature a 'Chef's salad'. Too often this is a combination of cold chicken, ham, cheese and wilted lettuce – put together by the staff who happen to be on duty when the real chef has gone to bed.

A cool vegetable dish needn't be like that. Planning in advance is not a bad idea and when you're entertaining it is sensible to choose one cold course. It balances the meal and needs no last-minute attention, leaving you free to concentrate on the hot dishes.

It isn't hard to make imaginative cold platters. It depends on using the freshest ingredients – the vegetables must never be tired if they are to look and taste good cold. I remember many cold tables that looked quite stunning but were disappointing to eat, with canned or frozen vegetables and cloying dressings.

The finished dishes should be cooled quickly and covered with clingfilm to keep them fresh. They should be taken out of the refrigerator at least 1 hour before a meal – most food is better cool, but not chilled.

Onions monegasque

Maybe this dish is named after the tiny country Monaco, because the onions are tiny too. One year I thought it would be marvellous to have a studio flat in the South of France, so I dragged my husband on a property search all over the Côte d'Azur. The one we found was ideal except for the price, but it was only as we were driving away that we realized we had just been in Monte Carlo!

450 g/1 lb small pickling onions
1 tbsp olive oil
1 tsp wine vinegar
1 tbsp tomato purée
15 g/½ oz sultanas
4 tbsp medium dry red or white wine
salt and pepper
pinch sugar (optional)

1 Peel the onions under cold running water and put them in a bowl with 150 ml/¼ pint boiling water. Cover and cook on HIGH for 6 minutes. Drain well.
2 Mix together the oil, vinegar, tomato purée, sultanas and wine and stir into the onions. Cook again for 2 minutes, and season with salt, pepper and sugar, if wished. Spoon over the tomato mixture and leave to cool.

Aubergine wedges

If you're tired of conventional looking salads, here's a dish which is completely disguised – most people will be intrigued but won't know what it is. The mayonnaise coating can be decorated as simply or elegantly as you wish. Cooking the mixture in a ring shape avoids the cold spot in the middle which takes longer to cook.

450 g/1 lb aubergines
2 large onions, chopped
2 tbsp olive oil
½ tsp sugar
1 tsp lemon juice
salt and pepper
1 egg, beaten
Garnish
4 tbsp thick mayonnaise
sliced radishes
sliced gherkins, stuffed olives or red pepper
    diamonds

1 Prick the aubergines and cook on HIGH for 5 minutes, or until soft. Leave to cool slightly, remove the seeds and scoop out the flesh.
2 Sauté the onions in the oil in a frying pan over high heat until brown. Put in a blender or food processor with the aubergine flesh, sugar, lemon juice and seasoning and process until the mixture is smooth. Stir in the egg.
3 Place an upturned cup in the centre of a shallow 22.5 cm/9 in round dish. Pour the mixture round the cup, smoothing it out to make it quite flat. Cook on MEDIUM (5) for about 7–8 minutes, or until the aubergine mixture is just coming away from the edges. Leave to cool and cut it into wedges.
4 Spoon over the mayonnaise, covering the surface completely, and garnish with thin slices of radish, gherkin slices, olives or red pepper diamond shapes.

Beetroot and smatana with crudités

Beetroot is the only vegetable you can buy already cooked – imagine those great cauldrons of bubbling red juice at the wholesale markets! In early summer you can buy bunches of raw baby beets with long stems and ruby-tipped leaves which make an interesting salad. Boiling in conventional pans is messy and slow, but for new beetroot here is a quick and worthwhile method.

450 g/1 lb small uncooked beetroots
175 ml/6 fl oz boiling water
salt
Smatana dips and crudités
300 ml/½ pint creamed smatana, Greek yogurt
*   or soured cream*
1 small avocado
pinch saffron or turmeric
2 carrots, cut into sticks
4 large spring onions, cut into brushes
½ cucumber, cut into sticks
few sticks celery, cut into fine sticks
100 g/4 oz French beans

1 Remove the leaves and stems and scrub the beetroot gently. Cut into quarters and put into a large dish. Pour in the boiling water, cover and cook on HIGH for 9 minutes. Lift the beetroot out with a slotted spoon, season and leave to cool slightly, then peel carefully.
2 To prepare the dips, divide the smatana, yogurt or cream between 4 pots. Mash the avocado with a fork and mix it into one quarter. Add the saffron to a tablespoon of boiling water, stir and leave to infuse for 10 minutes.
3 Strain a little of the liquid into another portion to turn it yellow. If using turmeric, simply stir it in. Swirl some beetroot over a third portion to make it marbled pink and leave the last one white.
4 Arrange the vegetables with the dips on a plate and serve with the beetroot.

Tortilla española – Spanish omelette

Spaniards don't eat dinner until about 10 p.m., but enjoy a huge variety of 'tapas' or snacks with a drink in the early evening. This is one of them – adapted for the microwave – that is equally good hot or cold.

1 tbsp olive oil
1 small onion, finely chopped
50 g/2 oz French beans, sliced
50 g/2 oz frozen or cooked fresh peas
2 boiled new potatoes, diced
salt and pepper
4 eggs

1 Heat the oil in a bowl on HIGH for 1 minute, then add the onion. Cook for 2–3 minutes, coating with the oil, until it softens.
2 Put the beans in a bowl with 1–2 tbsp water, cover and cook on HIGH for 2 minutes. Add the frozen peas and cook for 1 minute, or just stir in cooked peas, if using.
3 Season all the vegetables lightly and mix together in the base of a 15 cm/6 in round dish. Spread them out evenly.
4 Lightly whisk the eggs, add salt and pepper and pour over the cooked vegetables. Cook on MEDIUM (6) for 4 minutes, occasionally lifting the edges towards the middle to let the uncooked egg pour to the outside. Continue cooking for a further 2 minutes, making sure the centre is cooked.
5 Leave to cool slightly, then slide the omelette out on to a flat plate. Cut into small wedges when cold.

Summer vegetable platter

Chefs used to give their apprentices the tedious task of 'turning' vegetables. The point was to produce small, even-sized shapes, which cooked faster. The same principle applies with microwaving, so instead of cutting intricate shapes, you should make sure the vegetables are roughly the same size. The 'summer' taste depends on freshness, so look out for beans that snap when you bend them and potatoes with skins that rub off in your hands. Only peel the potatoes and carrots if you dislike the skins.

450 g/1 lb small new potatoes, scrubbed
salt and pepper
1 mint sprig
450 g/1 lb new carrots, scrubbed
120 ml/4 fl oz vegetable stock
425 g/15 oz young bobby or French beans,
  topped and tailed
200 g/7 oz small mange-tout, trimmed
To serve
Green Mayonnaise (p. 38) or Smatana with
Chives (p. 36) or Yogurt Herb Dip (see p. 41)

1 To save time while you are microwaving the other vegetables, cook the potatoes in a saucepan of salted boiling water with the mint until tender. Drain them well.
2 Meanwhile, cut the carrots into halves if large. Put them in a dish, sprinkle over 4 tbsp vegetable stock, cover and cook on HIGH for 6 minutes.
3 Cook the beans in the same way for 5½ minutes. Cook the mange-tout with no extra water or stock for 3 minutes.
4 Season all the vegetables after cooking and drain well. Arrange on a large flat dish.

Note: This makes enough for about 8 people. Keep the cooking liquid or freeze it in small pots for use in soups.

Summer vegetable platter with Green mayonnaise (see p. 38).

Salade niçoise

The Mayor of Nice has very definite ideas about what goes into an authentic Salade Niçoise. According to him, anchovies and olives are all right, but cooked beans and potatoes are not. Perhaps I should re-name my version 'Salade Provençale Micro-Onde'!

275 g/10 oz new potatoes, scrubbed
100 g/4 oz French beans, topped and tailed
salt and pepper
1 large crisp lettuce
350 g/12 oz tuna fish
4–6 anchovy fillets (see note below)
8 black olives
12 cherry tomatoes or 4 firm tomatoes, quartered
vinaigrette dressing, to serve

1 Cut the potatoes into slices unless they are very tiny. Put in a dish with 2 tbsp water, cover and cook on HIGH for 4 minutes.
2 Add the beans, re-cover and cook on HIGH for about 3 minutes (or slightly more if you like the vegetables softer). Drain, then sprinkle with a little salt and pepper.
3 Wash the lettuce and dry it very well. Line a large bowl with the leaves and pile the drained beans and potatoes in the centre. Flake the tuna and mix it in, then scatter over the anchovy fillets. Add the olives and tomatoes and mix everything roughly together.
4 Just before serving, toss with the vinaigrette dressing.

Note: To make anchovy fillets less salty, soak them in milk or water for 10 minutes, then drain.

Tossed salad with turbot and French beans

Don't despair if you can't get turbot. Any firm white fish like halibut will do, but cod and haddock tend to collapse when they are cut into small pieces.

550 g/1¼ lb turbot, filleted and skinned
50 ml/2 fl oz white wine
225 g/8 oz young French beans, topped and tailed
3 tbsp vegetable stock or water
1 crisp lettuce, such as Webb's or oakleaf
12 cherry tomatoes
75 g/3 oz small button mushrooms
1 clove garlic, crushed
6 tbsp olive oil
2 tbsp wine vinegar
½ tsp mustard
salt and pepper

1 Cut the turbot into large chunks or cubes, put in a dish and pour over the wine. Leave to stand while preparing the vegetables.
2 Put the beans in a dish, sprinkle with the stock, cover and cook on HIGH for 5 minutes (or longer if you like them soft). Drain and leave to cool.
3 Wash and dry the salad leaves, tomatoes and mushrooms.
4 Mix the garlic and oil in a small jar and cook on HIGH for 20 seconds. Leave to cool slightly, then add the vinegar, mustard and seasoning and shake the dressing very well.
5 Cover the fish and cook on HIGH for 1 minute, stir and cook again for another minute, or until it is opaque. Drain and leave to cool.
6 To assemble the salad, place the leaves on a large dish with the cooled fish in the centre. Arrange the beans, mushrooms and tomatoes around the fish and strain the dressing over the turbot (don't pour it all on, as it might be too much). Toss the salad and serve immediately.

Leek and corn rolls

In Sardinia there is clear blue sea, perfect sand and a hotel with a superb cold buffet. They used asparagus tips with melted cheese, served cold – my idea was to try the same with leeks and corn.

275 g/10 oz leeks, trimmed
200–225 ml/7–8 fl oz vegetable stock
25 g/1 oz butter
100 g/4 oz baby corn cobs
salt and pepper
50 g/2 oz Cheddar cheese

1 Cut off the green ends of the leeks, leaving the white part the same length as the corn cobs. Lay them flat and with a knife, make horizontal cuts to the centre of the white parts, taking care not to slice them right through. Open out the leeks and wash them very carefully and then drain.
2 Separate the layers of leek, put in a dish and sprinkle with 2 tbsp stock. Cover and cook on HIGH for 4 minutes, or until soft.
3 Chop the remaining pieces. Put half the butter in a bowl and cook on HIGH for 35 seconds, stir in the chopped leeks to coat them, then cook for about 4 minutes.
4 Sprinkle the corn cobs with 2 tbsp stock in a separate dish, cover and cook on HIGH for 1–2 minutes, depending on how crisp you like them. Toss in the rest of the butter.
5 Purée the chopped leeks in a blender or food processor with about 125–150 ml/4–5 fl oz stock until they make a fairly thick purée. Season to taste, but don't add too much salt.
6 Arrange the drained leek layers, with the purée down the centres and a corn cob on each one. Press up the sides to make open cylinders and arrange them fairly close together so they don't open.
7 Cut the cheese into thin strips and lay these over the leek rolls. Cook on HIGH for about 1 minute or until the cheese is just melted. Serve hot or cold.

Winter rice salad

Everyone has a favourite method of cooking rice – I actually prefer to boil it in masses of water and drain it frequently to get rid of all the starch. But if you want to be free to go and read a book for about 20 minutes, try this microwave method.

225 g/8 oz long-grain rice
600 ml/1 pint boiling water
¼ tsp salt
100 g/4 oz beans or peas
1 apple
3 sticks celery
juice of 1 lemon
Dressing
½ tsp curry powder
1 tbsp lemon juice
1 tsp golden syrup
salt and black pepper

1 Rinse the rice in cold water and put it in a large dish with the boiling water and salt. Stir it once, cover and cook on HIGH for 12 minutes. Leave to stand for another 10–11 minutes, then fluff it up with a fork and leave to cool slightly.
2 Put the beans or peas in a dish with 2–3 tbsp water, cover and cook on HIGH for 3–4 minutes, or until soft. Season lightly.
3 Cut the apple and celery into chunks and pour the lemon juice over the apple to stop it discolouring. Mix the rice with the vegetables and the drained apple.
4 To make the dressing, mix the curry powder with the lemon juice and golden syrup. Cook on HIGH for 30 seconds, then season. Leave to cool slightly, then pour it over the rice salad, carefully coating all the grains. Leave to cool.

Soft cheese and vegetable domes

Have you ever invited a friend who asked you *not* to cook? 'Just a plate of cottage cheese and a salad, please – I'm on a diet.' Here is something just as slimming but more fun.

225 g/8 oz skimmed milk soft cheese
2 small egg yolks
paprika and salt
50 g/2 oz cooked courgettes, diced
50 g/2 oz cooked carrots, diced
50 g/2 oz cooked sweetcorn kernels
50 g/2 oz cooked peas
To serve
Melba toast
green salad

1 Mix the soft cheese with the egg yolks in a food processor or beat until the mixture is quite smooth. Season with paprika and salt.
2 Mix together the courgettes, carrots, sweetcorn and peas.
3 Have ready 4 small 50 ml/2 fl oz ramekins and spoon a little cheese mixture into the bases. Spoon some of the vegetables into each one, reserving some for decoration. Cover with the rest of the cheese and level the tops. Bang the ramekins on the table to make sure there are no air gaps.
4 Arrange the ramekins around the outside of the turntable and cook on LOW (4) for 3–4 minutes, or until the mixture starts to come away from the sides. (It will continue cooking slightly as it cools.) Run a knife round the edges and carefully turn them out when they are cold.
5 Serve on individual plates with the rest of the mixed vegetables, Melba toast and a green salad.

Leek and corn rolls (see p. 97); Soft cheese and vegetable domes; Tossed salad with turbot and French beans (see p. 96).

Sliced aubergine salad

According to legend the Imam, or Turkish priest, fainted when he first ate a deliciously oily aubergine dish. Today it is the dietitians who are more likely to faint at the idea of so much oil. I expect the Imam's cook didn't have a microwave – otherwise he would have known how to reduce both the time and the oil in the famous recipe. He might even have been persuaded to try this salad.

450 g/1 lb aubergines
salt and pepper
3 cloves garlic, crushed
3 tbsp tomato purée
½ tsp sugar
2–3 tbsp olive oil
1 tbsp chopped fresh mint
1 tbsp chopped fresh parsley

1 Slice the aubergines into thin rounds and sprinkle with plenty of salt. Leave to drain on a wire rack over absorbent kitchen paper for about 20 minutes.
2 Preheat the oven to 200 C (400 F/Gas 6).
3 Make a paste of the crushed garlic, tomato purée, sugar, salt and pepper.
4 Rinse and dry the aubergines very well. Arrange in a dish and cook on HIGH for about 4 minutes.
5 Brush a sheet of foil or a baking tray with 1 tbsp oil and arrange the slices on it in a single layer. Spread a little paste over each one and sprinkle over the remaining oil. Bake in the oven for 10–15 minutes. Cool slightly, then lift the aubergine slices on to a serving dish. Sprinkle with the chopped herbs and serve either warm or cold.

Courgette and mushroom ring

The very centre of the microwave turntable is in fact a 'cold spot' and unless you position food carefully, or stir it, the middle is often uncooked. You can avoid this by cooking dishes like this in a ring mould, but if you don't have one, here's a good use for your food processer bowl with its central tube.

450 g/1 lb large courgettes
100 g/4 oz cauliflower florets
50–75 ml/2–3 fl oz dark beef or mushroom
  stock
1½ tbsp oil
175 g/6 oz mushrooms, chopped
1 tbsp plain flour
salt and pepper
1 egg white

1 Cut off the ends of the courgettes, then cut them lengthwise into thin slices with a vegetable parer. Put the slices in a dish, cover and cook on HIGH for 1 minute with no water. Chop the remaining pieces and cook them for about 2 minutes, or until they are soft.
2 Cut the cauliflower into very small pieces and put in a dish with 3 tbsp stock, cover and cook on HIGH for 4 minutes.
3 Put ½ tbsp oil in a bowl and cook on HIGH for 40 seconds, add the mushrooms, stirring to coat in the oil, then cook on HIGH for about 3 minutes. Stir in the flour to make a thick paste and slowly add about 50 ml/2 fl oz dark stock. Cook for about 1 minute, stirring until the mushroom mixture is very thick. Leave to cool slightly, fold in the other vegetable pieces and season well.
4 Arrange the courgette slices in a 17.5 cm/7 in ring mould or food processor bowl overlapping them slightly and making sure they are even lengths. If necessary, narrow the ends so that the slices overlap neatly at the centre. Reserve some pieces for the top.
5 Whisk the egg white lightly, then fold it

into the vegetable mixture. Pour it into the lined mould and cover the top with the courgette slices, folding over the side pieces. Cook, uncovered, on MEDIUM for about 5 minutes, or until the filling seems firm and not liquid. Leave to cool slightly, then run a knife round the edges to loosen the sides.
6 Put a plate over the top and carefully turn it out, rearranging any courgette slices which have slipped out of place. Leave to cool completely with a few sheets of absorbent kitchen paper over the top to absorb any extra juice. Brush the ring with the remaining oil to make it glossy, then serve cold cut in wedges.

Pasta, peppers and peas

Leftover cooked pasta can be brought to life again with the bright colours and oily juices of the peppers. You can add extra crunch with toasted sunflower seeds or chopped celery, and if you are a garlic lover, you can always include some crushed cloves when you are heating the oil.

1–2 tbsp olive oil
275 g/10 oz yellow and orange peppers, cut into thin rings
salt and pepper
425 g/15 oz cooked pasta bows or shells
175 g/6 oz shelled peas, cooked

1 Heat half the oil in a dish on HIGH for 1 minute. Add the peppers and toss to coat with the oil. Cook on HIGH for 3 minutes, stirring once and adding more oil if they start to get dry. Season well.
2 Put the pasta and peas into a deep bowl, pour over the peppers with their juice and fold everything together. Taste again for seasoning and serve either warm or cold.

Note: If using raw pasta, you will need to cook about 175 g/6 oz.

Green cauliflower salad

The intricate spiral patterns on these autumn vegetables are as beautiful as any flower. Microwaving keeps the light green colour and contrasting textures can be introduced with celeriac or late runner beans. I have used strips of carrot and courgette which can be curled attractively.

1 green cauliflower
6 tbsp vegetable stock
2 carrots, peeled
2 courgettes, trimmed
salt and pepper
To serve
Walnut Vinaigrette (see p. 16) or Mayonnaise (see p. 38 or 41).

1 Separate the cauliflower into florets of an even size. Discard the outer stalks and dark leaves – reserve the white stalks for soup.
2 Wash and drain the florets and arrange them in a single layer in a shallow dish. Sprinkle over 4 tbsp vegetable stock, cover and cook on HIGH for 5 minutes. (Test after 4 if you prefer the cauliflower crisp). Drain and leave to cool.
3 Cut the carrots and courgettes into thin strips with a vegetable parer and roll into curls, securing with a cocktail stick (see p. 82). Put the carrots in a dish with the remaining stock, cover and cook on HIGH for 1–2 minutes. Put the courgettes in a dish with no liquid, cover and cook for about 1 minute.
4 Arrange the cauliflower florets on a decorative plate with the carrot and courgette strips, season lightly and serve cool but not chilled, accompanied by vinaigrette or mayonnaise.

Summer rice salad

It is a good idea to cook extra quantities of plain rice or pasta to keep for a few days in the refrigerator. You can transform it quickly into an imaginative salad by adding it to some cooked, hot vegetables and leaving it to cool to develop the flavours. Follow the basic rule of doubling the quantities of things you like and leaving out those you don't.

2 tbsp oil
2 orange or yellow peppers, cut into squares or
   diamonds
6 large spring onions, sliced
150 g/5 oz small button mushrooms
350 g/12 oz cooked white rice
salt and black pepper
6 fresh mint leaves

1 Put half the oil in a shallow dish and cook on HIGH for 40 seconds. Add the peppers and cook on HIGH for 2 minutes, stirring once or twice.
2 Add the spring onions and cook for 1–2 minutes.
3 Stir in the small mushrooms with the rest of the oil and cook for 1–2 minutes, or until the juices start to run.
4 Immediately, fold in the cooked rice while the mixture is hot and season well to taste.
5 Finely chop half the mint leaves and stir into the salad. Spoon into a bowl and scatter over the rest of the mint.

Aubergine wedges (see p. 92); Onions monegasque (see p. 92); Summer rice salad.

Shallots in wine with red peppers

Shallots are milder than onions and should never be fried as it makes them bitter. Cooking them lightly in oil and then wine brings out a delicate flavour which goes well with cold meat and poultry.

20 shallots
2–3 tbsp oil
1 red pepper, deseeded and cut into thin slices or
rings
1 tsp brown sugar
salt and pepper
75 ml/3 fl oz white wine

1 Peel the shallots under running water and dry with absorbent paper.
2 Heat the oil in a dish on HIGH for 1½ minutes. Add the shallots and cook for 2 minutes, stirring once or twice to coat with the oil. Add the pepper slices or rings and cook for 2 minutes.
3 Remove the pepper slices and arrange round the side of a small dish. Sprinkle the shallots with the sugar, salt and pepper and pour over the wine. Cook on HIGH for a further 2 minutes, when the shallots should be quite tender.
4 Lift out the shallots with a slotted spoon and pile them in the centre of the dish. If the juice looks thin, reduce it in the microwave by cooking, uncovered, on HIGH for a further 2 minutes. Pour it over the shallots and leave to cool.

Baby corn, broccoli and cheese salad

This is a salad of contrasts – a smooth dressing with crunchy vegetables, and pale yellow with striking green.

175 g/6 oz baby corn cobs
4 tbsp vegetable stock or water
salt and pepper
225 g/8 oz broccoli
1 tbsp walnut oil
1 very small head celery, cut into even-sized
pieces
3–4 tbsp soured cream or smatana
75 g/3 oz bel paese, jarlsberg or gouda cheese,
cubed
paprika

1 Put the corn cobs in a dish and sprinkle with 2 tbsp stock or water. Cover and cook on HIGH for 4 minutes. Drain, salt lightly and leave to cool.
2 Arrange the broccoli in a dish with the heads pointing towards the centre, add remaining stock or water, cover and cook on HIGH for 3–4 minutes, depending on whether you like them crisp or soft. Drain and toss in the oil with a little salt.
3 Just before serving, arrange some of the corn cobs, broccoli and celery around the outside of a round dish. Toss the rest with the soured cream or smatana and cheese, sprinkle with paprika and pile into the centre.

Vegetable terrine with mousseline of fish

When you cook different coloured vegetable 'sticks' in a terrine, the effect is stunning, but you need something to hold it all together. You can either use minced fish, as in this recipe, or chicken – either of them provides a contrast in both colour and texture. Start early in the day so that the terrine is thoroughly chilled before you attempt to slice it.

350 g/12 oz boned and filleted salmon trout
175 ml/6 fl oz single or whipping cream
2 tbsp lemon juice
2 egg whites
salt and pepper
175 g/6 oz carrots
175 g/6 oz courgettes
100 g/4 oz French beans, topped and tailed
150 ml/¼ pint vegetable stock
Tomato Vinaigrette (see p. 41) or Greek
*   yogurt, to serve*

1 Put the fish in the bowl of a food processor with the cream. Process slowly, gradually adding the lemon juice and the egg whites. When the mixture is smooth, add the seasoning (slightly more than you would expect because the cream makes it quite bland), then chill the mixture in the refrigerator.
2 Cut the carrots and courgettes lengthwise into slices and then again into long sticks. Cook the vegetables separately, covered: cook the carrots with 3 tbsp stock in a bowl on HIGH for 4 minutes, the beans with 2 tbsp stock for 4 minutes and the courgettes with 2 tbsp stock for 2 minutes. Pour off any liquid and leave the sticks to cool.
3 Spoon a quarter of the fish mixture over the base of a 600 ml/1 pint glass terrine dish. Arrange the vegetables in separate layers – first the courgettes, then some fish, then the carrots, more fish and finally the beans.

Spread the remaining fish mixture over the top, cover and cook on MEDIUM (3) for 4 minutes. Leave to stand for 5 minutes, then carefully pour off some of the juices. Invert the terrine over a plate and leave to cool. Drain again and chill in the refrigerator for at least 3 hours.
4 Slice the terrine and arrange it with small piles of any remaining vegetables around the dish. Serve with Tomato Vinaigrette or Greek yogurt.

Note: As microwave cookers vary in power, it may be necessary to adjust the timing of this terrine. The edges should just come away from the sides when it is cooked. The top should feel just set after the standing time. Remember you can always cook it a little more, but longer cooking than necessary will make the fish mixture tough.

Aubergine and tomato salad

This version of aubergine salad is made using a combination cooker.

350 g/12 oz aubergines
salt and pepper
5 tbsp olive oil
3 cloves garlic, crushed
2 large tomatoes, thinly sliced

1 Prepare the aubergines as for Sliced Aubergine Salad (p. 100), making sure they are well rinsed and dried.
2 Arrange the slices in a single layer in a large round dish. Sprinkle over half the olive oil mixed with the crushed garlic and season well.
3 Arrange the tomato slices over the aubergine rounds. Drizzle over the rest of the oil and cook on COMBINATION 8 (250C 275W) for about 25 minutes. Serve either warm or cold.

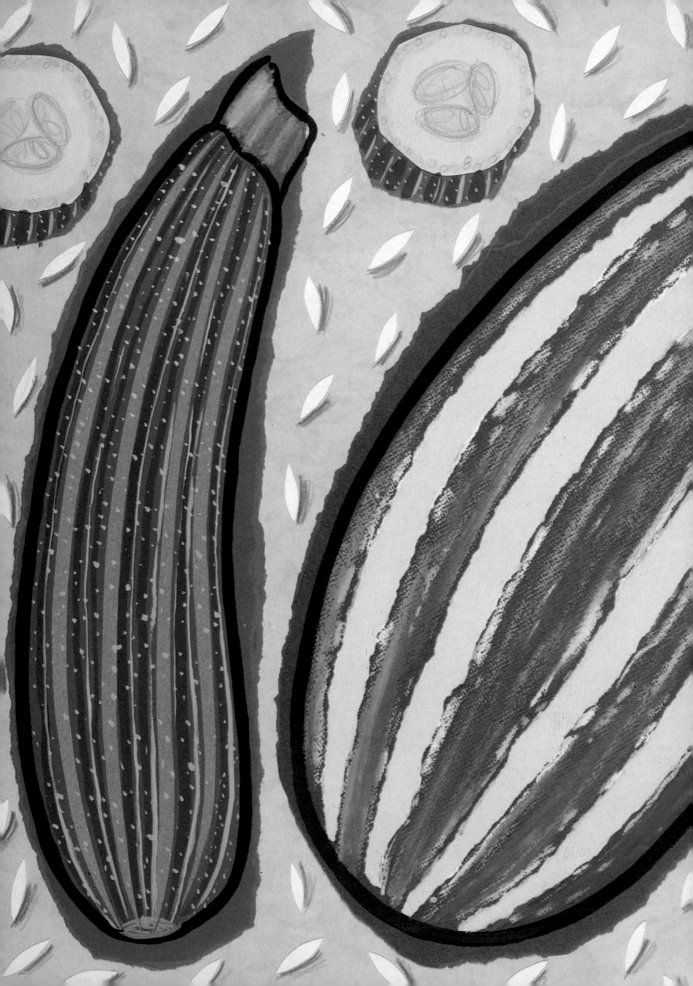

Stuffed Vegetables

Most adventurous cuisines were born out of poverty. Peasant dishes of the Middle and Far East were often based on rice, vegetables and spices. Traditional Jewish cooks devised some marvellous stuffed dishes to supplement small amounts of meat or fish. This was because meat and poultry were expensive and, for inland communities, fish was often unobtainable. In Mrs Beeton's England, stuffing was usually a forcemeat mixture of minced meat, herbs and breadcrumbs. Without the constraints of shortages, ideas about stuffings have changed. They can be made with anything you like: dates with meat, nuts with cheese, herbs and spices with rice, or almost any combination you care to invent. Vegetables make perfect natural containers. They are easy to serve as they form individual 'portions' and they look stunning if filled with contrasting colours and textures. Many of these dishes can be prepared early and reheated successfully. In a normal oven, the vegetables would go brown at the edges and the fillings would dry up. The microwave keeps the colours bright and the stuffings moist – as fresh, several hours later, as when you first put it together.

Hot spiced onions with raita

Braised onions normally take an hour to soften. Using a frying pan for the colour and the microwave for speed reduces the time to 20 minutes. Add more spices if you like a stronger curry flavour – and even sprinkle some over the raita – though I prefer it to be cool and mild.

700 g/1½ lb onions, halved
225 g/8 oz potatoes, peeled and diced
2 tbsp oil
½ tsp paprika
½ tsp cumin
¼ tsp each chilli powder, turmeric and garam masala, optional
50 g/2 oz frozen peas
salt
Cucumber raita
100 g/4 oz cucumber
½ tsp grated onion
150 ml/¼ pint low-fat natural yogurt

1 Put the onions in a shallow dish, cover and cook on HIGH for 6 minutes. Turn them over and continue cooking for another 4 minutes.
2 Put the potatoes in a separate dish with a little boiling water, cover and cook on HIGH for 4–5 minutes, until tender. Drain.
3 Remove the centres of the onions and chop the flesh roughly. Season.
4 Heat the oil in a frying pan on the stove and sauté the onion shells until turning brown. Transfer to a round dish. Sauté the chopped onion and sprinkle over the spices, stirring well for a few minutes.
5 Defrost the peas slightly in the microwave and add them, with any juice, and the cooked potatoes to the spice mixture. Taste for seasoning.
6 Fill the centres of the halved onions with the mixture and arrange in a dish. Pile any extra mixture into the centre of the dish. Deglaze the frying pan with a few tablespoons of water and sprinkle this over the onions. Cover and cook on HIGH for 4

minutes. The water will have evaporated and the onions can be served hot or cold.
7 For the raita, grate the cucumber on to absorbent kitchen paper and squeeze out the juice. Stir the grated cucumber and onion into the yogurt and season to taste. Serve chilled.

Yellow peppers with bulghur

It's tempting to use green, yellow and red peppers for colour, but remember that green ones are unripe and therefore not as sweet. Bulghur is partially cooked cracked wheat and is much favoured in Middle Eastern cooking.

4–6 yellow, orange or red peppers
3 tbsp olive oil
½ onion, finely chopped
100 g/4 oz bulghur
225 ml/8 fl oz strong chicken or vegetable stock
5 apricots (fresh or pre-soaked, dried)
salt and pepper
25 g/1 oz shelled pistachio nuts, skinned and sliced

1 Cut the tops off the peppers. Remove the seeds and membranes in the centre, then wash the peppers and dry carefully.
2 Stand the peppers upright in a dish and cook on HIGH for 3 minutes. Add half the olive oil and cook again for 2 minutes. Watch to see that the tops are not getting overcooked and remove after 1 minute if they seem soft. Season. Drain off the oily liquid and reserve.
3 Heat 1 tbsp oil in a large bowl on HIGH for 40 seconds. Add the chopped onion, stir and cook for 2 minutes.
4 Wash and drain the bulghur very well, then add to the onions and cook on HIGH for 30 seconds.
5 Pour in twice its volume of stock and cook on HIGH for 2 minutes, stirring occasionally.

Leave to stand so that the bulghur absorbs the rest of the liquid.

6 Stone the apricots if using fresh, then cut them into strips. Put them in a dish and cook on HIGH for 1 minute.

7 Taste the bulghur for seasoning, mix in the apricots and nuts and spoon the mixture into the peppers. Replace the tops, trickle over the rest of the oil mixed with the reserved oily juice and cook on HIGH for 1 minute. Serve warm or cold.

Variation: If preferred, place the peppers on their sides and slice off about one-third for lids. Cut a thin slice from the opposite side of each pepper to make a flat surface to enable the pepper to stay upright.

Stuffed cabbage leaves with mushroom duxelles

Summer vegetables of the Mediterranean aren't the only good 'containers'. Everyday winter vegetables can also be stuffed and need only a velvety sauce to transform them into a main course dish.

8 cabbage leaves
salt and pepper
2 tbsp oil
1 large onion, finely chopped
225 g/8 oz mushrooms, finely chopped
75 g/3 oz French or runner beans, finely
  chopped
75 g/3 oz cooked rice
150 g/5 oz cooked or canned borlotti beans,
  drained
1–2 tbsp soy sauce
2 tbsp sherry
Celeriac Sauce (see p. 37), to serve

1 Put the cabbage leaves in a dish, cover and cook on HIGH for 1 minute. Sprinkle with salt and pepper, shake the dish, then pat the leaves dry with absorbent kitchen paper.

2 Heat 1 tbsp oil in a frying pan and sauté the chopped onion over high heat until it starts to brown. Add the mushrooms, with a little more oil if necessary, and continue cooking until the mixture is brown. Season.

3 Put the green beans in a small dish, cover and cook on HIGH for 1½ minutes. Season with a little salt.

4 Mix half the mushroom mixture with the green beans and the rice. Stir in the borlotti beans.

5 Spread out the cabbage leaves and place a large spoonful of the filling into each one. Turn in the sides and roll over to form parcels. Arrange them round a dish with the smoothest part of the leaf upwards.

6 Pour the soy sauce and sherry into the remaining mushroom mixture, turn up the heat and cook for about 1 minute. Pour the mixture over the cabbage leaves and cook, uncovered, on HIGH for 2 minutes.

7 Serve immediately, surrounded by a pool of celeriac sauce.

Note: You can prepare this dish in advance but you will then need to heat it for longer to make sure the filling is hot.

Cabbage rolls with chestnut filling

Chestnuts and sprouts are a classic combination with the Christmas turkey. For those who loathe sprouts here is a much more original idea.

1 winter green cabbage (about 16 leaves)
1 tbsp oil
1 onion
350 g/12 oz chestnut purée
25 g/1 oz toasted cashew nuts
salt and pepper
3 tbsp turkey or chicken gravy

1 Cut a cone out of the base of the cabbage so that the leaves come away and wash them very well. Put them in a large bowl and cover with plenty of boiling water. Leave for a few minutes until they have softened slightly, then drain and pat dry.
2 Heat the oil in a small saucepan and sauté the chopped onion over high heat until it is golden brown. Deglaze the pan with a tbsp water and cook for another minute.
3 Mix the onion with the puréed chestnut and fold in the toasted nuts. Season to taste with salt and pepper.
4 Lay out the cabbage leaves and put a heaped spoonful of the chestnut mixture into each one. Roll them up into neat parcels, folding in the edges and making sure the filling is completely enclosed. Arrange them fairly closely in a single layer in a shallow dish.
5 When the roast turkey or chicken is ready, spoon off some of the gravy and sprinkle a little over the cabbage rolls. Cook on HIGH for about 3 minutes, or until they are very hot. Spoon over a little more gravy and serve immediately.

Cabbage rolls with chestnut stuffing; Hot spiced onions with raita (see p. 108); Stuffed cabbage leaves with mushroom duxelles (see p. 109).

Spinach 'quiche' boats

You can hardly have a vegetable book without a quiche! Pastry bases often get soggy, so here is an idea based on Michel Guérard's earliest experiments with 'cuisine minceur'. The joy of microwaving is that you can try out all kinds of containers – I used glass avocado dishes because they make a nice 'boat' shape, but small cereal bowls would do instead. Since small quantities cook quicker (and I only have four dishes!), cook half the boats, then repeat with the rest of the filling.

225 g/8 oz large-leafed spinach
150 g/5 oz cream cheese
2 whole eggs
2 egg yolks
4 spring onions, finely chopped
100 g/4 oz Cheddar cheese, grated
salt and pepper

1 Wash the spinach well and shake it dry. Cut off the stalks and arrange a few leaves at a time on a plate. (Be careful not to bruise or split them.) Cook on HIGH for 30 seconds or until the leaves are slightly soft. Drain and pat dry with absorbent kitchen paper.
2 Mix the cream cheese with the whole eggs and yolks. Stir the onions into the mixture with the grated cheese. Taste for seasoning and add pepper and a little salt.
3 Line 4 glass or china dishes with whole spinach leaves, leaving them to overlap the edges slightly. Using half the cheese mixture, spoon some into the centre of each leaf and cook on MEDIUM (3) for 2 minutes. Stir the filling gently as the edges cook quicker, then cook for another 2–3 minutes. Leave to stand for a few minutes when the filling will be just set. Fold over the edges of the spinach leaves and slide the 'boats' out on to a plate.
4 Repeat with the rest of the spinach and filling and serve the quiches warm or cold.

Tomatoes stuffed with spaghetti squash

Years ago, when 'real' spaghetti was hardly known in England, a television presenter played an elaborate joke on viewers by showing scenes of the Italian spaghetti harvest. A new vegetable now on the market is almost as unbelievable. The spaghetti squash, yellow, hard and oval like a melon, produces spaghetti-like strands when cooked. Although you could hardly eat a whole plate of it like pasta, it responds well to the butter and Parmesan treatment and is a good filling for cooked tomatoes or peppers.

1 spaghetti squash
salt and pepper
25 g/1 oz butter
4 large tomatoes, weighing about 350 g/12 oz, halved
1 tbsp tomato purée
25–50 g/1–2 oz freshly grated Parmesan

1 First prepare the spaghetti squash. Slice it in half horizontally and scoop out the seeds and the soft membranes. Sprinkle with a few tablespoons of boiling water, cover and cook one half on HIGH for 6 minutes. (Reserve the other half for another time.)
2 Holding it with a towel, take a fork and scrape the flesh into strands and pile the 'spaghetti' into a bowl. Season well with salt and pepper and stir in the butter. Keep warm while you prepare the tomatoes.
3 Put the tomatoes in a dish, cover and cook on HIGH for 2 minutes. Scoop out the centres and mash the tomato pulp with the tomato purée, and plenty of salt and pepper. Strain this sauce into a bowl.
4 Fill the tomato shells with the spaghetti squash, reheat on HIGH for about 1 minute (too long and the tomatoes will collapse). Serve on heated plates with a sprinkling of freshly grated cheese and a spoonful of the sauce on the side.

Marrow stuffed with minced beef

Few people adore marrow, unless they grow them by the dozen and learn to love them. What puts them off is the thought of sodden, tasteless flesh submerged in insipid white sauce. But it can be very different – microwaving reduces the water content and helps you make a quick savoury meat filling that goes well with rice or beans.

900 g/2 lb marrow
salt and pepper
350 g/12 oz lean minced beef
2 onions, finely chopped
2 tsp tomato purée
1 beef stock cube
Spanish Rice with Tomatoes (see p. 84), to serve

1 Cut the marrow in half horizontally (making a scalloped edge if you feel artistic). Scoop out the seeds and sprinkle over plenty of salt. Leave to drain upside-down over a bowl while preparing the meat filling.
2 Sauté the beef in a non-stick frying pan and add the onions when the fat starts to run. Cook over fairly high heat until both start to brown.
3 Transfer to a microwave dish, add the tomato purée and crumble over the stock cube, being careful to mix it in well. Season with pepper. Deglaze the frying pan with 3 tbsp boiling water and pour this into the meat mixture. Cover and cook on MEDIUM for 15 minutes.
4 Drain and dry the marrow and cook, covered, on HIGH for about 8 minutes or until tender. Drain off any more water, dry with absorbent kitchen paper and fill the marrow halves with the meat mixture. Reheat on HIGH until the marrow and filling are hot. Serve with Spanish rice.

Note: This dish can be prepared in advance and reheated later.

Cucumber trunks with dill and fish salad

Chunks of cucumber can sometimes be watery, so microwaving them briefly gets rid of some of the moisture but keeps the crunch and colour. Don't put the filling in too early as it will make them go soggy.

2 large cucumbers
Fish salad
½ spring onion, chopped
bunch fresh dill
salt and pepper
50 ml/2 fl oz milk
450 g/1 lb fresh cod fillet, skinned
175 g/6 oz cooked broad beans (about 700 g/
*   1½ lb in pods)*
4 tbsp mayonnaise
2 tbsp whipped cream

1 First prepare the cooking liquid for the fish salad. Put the spring onion with a few sprigs of dill in a jug, season and mix in the milk. Cook on HIGH for 30 seconds, then leave to infuse while it cools.
2 Meanwhile, make thin lines along the cucumbers with a fork and cut them into 5 cm/2 in lengths. Scoop out the centre seeds with a sharp knife. Salt and stand on absorbent paper for about 20 minutes.
3 Put the fish in a shallow dish, strain the milk over, cover and cook on HIGH for about 1 minute. Flake the fish and continue cooking for another minute, or until it is opaque. Leave to cool and drain in a colander.
4 Dry the cucumbers with absorbent kitchen paper and cook on HIGH, uncovered, for 2 minutes. Stand the shells on more paper and keep covered so that the moisture is absorbed while they cool.
5 Mix the flaked fish with the cooked beans, mayonnaise and cream and season well. Spoon the filling into the cucumber 'trunks' and stand them upright on a serving dish. Garnish with sprigs of dill.

Artichokes with tomato and lemon mousseline

Scraping off the flesh from artichokes seems tedious, but my mother would disagree – and at 86 she is still the best cook I know. Here is an idea from one of her superb meals.

4 large globe artichokes
4 large tomatoes
1 tbsp oil
salt and pepper
pinch sugar
5 tbsp lemon juice
2 egg yolks

1 Prepare and cook the artichokes (see p. 17), removing the hairy chokes from the centre.
2 Reserve some of the inside leaves and pull off enough to leave the heart quite visible from the top (taking about 8 leaves from each artichoke). With a pointed spoon, scrape the flesh off the wide end of each leaf and put it into a bowl.
3 Skin the tomatoes (see p. 20) and chop them roughly. Put the oil in a dish and cook on HIGH for 1 minute, add the tomatoes and cook for 2 minutes. Season with salt, pepper and a little sugar and continue cooking for another minute. Stir in 1 tbsp lemon juice and the artichoke flesh.
4 Reheat the artichokes briefly and keep them warm in a covered dish.
5 Mix the egg yolks with the remaining juice in a bowl and cook on MEDIUM (5) for 20 seconds. Stir well, cook for another 20 seconds or until the sauce starts to thicken slightly. (Be very careful that it does not turn to scrambled egg.) Stir the lemon sauce into the tomato and artichoke mixture and press it all through a strainer. Season, spoon into artichokes and keep warm.

Cucumber trunks with dill and fish salad (see p. 113); Artichokes with tomato and lemon mousseline.

Stuffed vine leaves

22 vine leaves
1 tbsp tomato purée
120 ml/4 fl oz tomato juice
½ tsp sugar
Rice filling
140 g/4 ½ oz long-grain rice
1 tbsp olive oil
2 spring onions, chopped
15 g/½ oz sultanas
salt and pepper
1 tbsp chopped fresh mint
¼ tsp ground cinnamon
¼ tsp grated nutmeg

1 First make the rice filling so that it will be cool enough to handle. Soak the rice in boiling water for a few minutes and rinse well to remove excess starch. Drain well.
2 Heat the oil in a large dish and cook on HIGH for 1 minute. Add the spring onions and cook for 40 seconds.
3 Add the rice, stir and pour in 250 ml/9 fl oz boiling water. Cover and cook on HIGH for 7 minutes.
4 Stir in the sultanas, salt and pepper and 65 ml/2½ fl oz water. Cook on HIGH for 3 minutes, then mix in the mint, cinnamon and nutmeg and taste for seasoning.
5 Pour boiling water over fresh vine leaves or carefully separate and rinse ones which come in a packet with brine. Dry them very well and arrange, with the stalk end towards you and the dull side up.
6 Place a spoonful of the rice in the centre of each leaf, fold in the sides and roll it forward to make a neat parcel. Be careful not to put in too much filling. Arrange the stuffed leaves close together, in a single layer, in a round shallow dish.
7 Mix together the tomato purée, juice, sugar and seasoning and pour this over the vine leaves. Cover and cook for about 4 minutes. The liquid should be almost absorbed. Leave to cool.

Spinach parcels with liver pâté

I first saw these in one of the best restaurants in the country. My idea was to tie them with leek strips and microwave them.

275 g/10 oz chicken or duck livers
1 tbsp oil
1 onion, finely chopped
600 ml/1 pint chicken consommé
salt and pepper
450 g/1 lb fresh spinach

1 First make the chicken liver pâté. Preheat the conventional grill. Wash the livers and remove any grisly bits. Pat them dry with absorbent kitchen paper, then grill for about 4 minutes on one side. Turn them over and continue for another minute.
2 Heat the oil in a small frying pan, add the onion and cook over high heat until the onion starts to brown, then pour in 1 tbsp chicken consommé.
3 In a blender or food processor, process the chicken livers with the onion. Season well and add another tablespoon of consommé if the mixture is very stiff. (You should be able to spoon it out but it should not be too liquid.) Leave the pâté to cool.
4 Cut off the spinach stalks and wash the leaves carefully. Choose about 20 of the best leaves, arrange a few at a time on a plate and cook on HIGH for about 30 seconds, or until they start to wilt.
5 Lay the leaves out on absorbent kitchen paper, pat them dry, then put about a teaspoonful of cooled pâté into the centre of each one. Fold in the sides and roll them over to make small parcels and arrange them, seam side down, in a shallow dish. Cover and chill.
6 To serve, spoon over 2 tbsp consommé, cover and cook the parcels on HIGH for 2 minutes. Have ready bowls of steaming hot consommé and carefully lift the parcels into the bowls. (This quantity makes about 20 small parcels.)

Jacket potatoes with creamy corn filling

No microwave book would be complete without the inevitable jacket potatoes! A combination cooker will brown the tops but if you don't have one, a grill will do fine. If preferred, use mushrooms, white fish or cheese and spinach instead of the corn.

2 large baking potatoes
50 g/2 oz butter
75 ml/3 fl oz milk
salt and pepper
15 g/½ oz plain flour
100 g/4 oz sweetcorn kernels, cooked

1 Bake the potatoes in the microwave according to their size, about 12 minutes on HIGH or slightly longer on COMBINATION 1 (250C 160W) if you want crisper skins.
2 Scoop out the centres and mix with half the butter and 25 ml/1 fl oz milk. Season well and when it is slightly cool spoon the creamed potato into a piping bag fitted with a shell nozzle.
3 Make a béchamel sauce (see p. 32) with the rest of the butter, flour and remaining milk and cook on HIGH for about 2 minutes, or until thick. Stir in the corn with a few tablespoons of the cooking juice so that the sauce is creamy. Divide the mixture into 4 and spoon it into the empty potato shells.
4 Pipe the creamed potato over the top in a lattice pattern and arrange the filled potatoes in a suitable round container.
5 Cook on COMBINATION 7 (250C 40W) for 15 minutes. Alternatively cook on HIGH for 3–4 minutes and brown the tops of the potatoes under a preheated grill.

Note: This makes 4 potato halves – enough for 2 or 4 depending on their appetites.

Aubergines with lamb

This is a popular combination in the Middle East. You can vary the spices or add lemon juice or chopped tomato if you wish. Salt, rinse and microwave the aubergine shells and flesh first to get rid of the bitter juices.

4 small aubergines, weighing about 575 g/ 1¼ lb
450 g/1 lb lamb from the leg or shoulder, cut into cubes
3 tbsp olive oil
2 onions, quartered
2 cloves garlic, crushed
pinch cumin
salt and pepper
1 tsp soy sauce
150 ml/¼ pint beef stock
1 tbsp chopped fresh coriander
boiled rice or green lentils, to serve

1 First prepare the aubergine shells (see p. 100, steps 1–4). Then sauté the aubergine cubes in some of the oil and remove with a slotted spoon.
2 Sauté the lamb cubes over high heat in a non-stick frying pan, until they start to brown and release some fat. Pour in the remaining oil, add the onions and garlic and cook until both the lamb and onions are brown. Sprinkle over the cumin, a little salt and pepper and deglaze the pan with the soy sauce and beef stock.
3 Transfer the meat and onions, with the stock, to a dish, cover and cook on MEDIUM for 15 minutes. Add the cubed aubergine and continue cooking on LOW (SIMMER) for about 10 minutes, or until the meat is tender.
4 Spoon the mixture into the aubergine shells, reheat for a few minutes and sprinkle with chopped coriander. Serve with boiled rice or green lentils.

Courgettes with pine nuts and lemon sauce

What used to be classed as an unusual vegetable has now become commonplace. So much so that one day, my little son, reading a story about a giant marrow, asked 'what's that, is it a very big courgette?'

450 g/1 lb courgettes
1 tbsp oil
salt and pepper
100 g/4 oz cooked brown or white rice (see note below)
100 g/4 oz canned borlotti beans, drained
50 g/2 oz roasted pine nuts
lemon sauce (see p. 33), to serve

1 Cut the courgettes in half horizontally and scoop out the centres.
2 Heat the oil in a shallow dish on HIGH for 40 seconds. Add the courgette halves and cook for 4 minutes, stirring once. Sprinkle with salt and pepper, then arrange them on a serving dish.
3 Put the chopped courgette flesh in a dish and cook on HIGH for 1 minute, then stir in the cooked rice and beans. Spoon the filling into the courgette shells and sprinkle with the roasted nuts. Serve hot or cold with lemon sauce.

Note: 40 g/1½ oz uncooked rice makes about 100 g/4 oz cooked.

Yellow peppers with bulghur (see p. 108); Jacket Potatoes with creamy corn filling (see p. 117); Courgettes with pine nuts and lemon sauce.

Entertaining

There is a great myth about entertaining. It all started with those elaborate menus aimed at 'impressing the boss'. I have a recipe from 1973 for 'Koor-jet fahr-see oh-sah-mohn' (or *courgettes farcies aux amandes*). I suppose the idea was that if you could find an unusual dish *and* pronounce it too you were certain to dazzle your guests.

Entertaining today is less daunting since most people take a far more relaxed view of it. A journalist I know always invites his friends at short notice. When they arrive, they sit down in the kitchen and he starts to prepare the food. An hour or so later he produces a wonderful soufflé, a perfectly dressed salad and a huge crème caramel. His friends talk to him while he does it all and the chaotic trail of dirty dishes and discarded debris doesn't worry any of them.

If you are a less confident cook, you will prefer to plan a selection of different dishes you are good at, rather than slaving over an impossibly complicated experiment. But whatever you choose, you can use your microwave to help you with the advance preparation.

Vegetable dishes are perfect for occasions of all kinds – from a simple lunch to a large buffet supper. I once invited some friends to an informal Sunday evening meal. Before we went in to eat one of the guests was telling me how he disliked vegetarian food and needed to have large quantities of fish or meat on his plate. I think he had changed his mind by the end of the evening, or perhaps he was too contentedly full to realize that every single dish was dominated by vegetables.

SUGGESTIONS FOR VEGETARIANS

Most of the recipes in this book about vegetables are suitable for vegetarians. Here are some suggested alternatives for dishes which contain fish or meat.

Courgette and Lamb Moussakas (see p.66)
Use grated cheese instead of minced lamb and vegetable stock instead of chicken stock.

Beef Salad (see p.66)
Leave out the cubes of meat and substitute smoked tofu.

Mange-tout Salad with Avocado and Smoked Turkey (see p.72)
Pile some cooked broad beans and toasted cashew nuts in the place of the smoked meat.

Salade Niçoise (see p.96)
Use chunks of cheese, avocado or artichoke hearts instead of the tuna.

Aubergines with Lamb (see p.117)
Fill the aubergine shells with a ratatouille mixture (see Crêpes Provençales p.72).

Marrow Stuffed with Minced Beef (see p.117)
Use the filling for Courgettes with Pine Nuts (p.118) instead of the minced meat.

Cucumber Trunks with Dill and Fish Salad (see p.113)
Change the filling to Winter or Summer Rice Salad (p.97 or 102).

Spinach Parcels with Liver Pâté (see p.116)

Fill the parcels with Almond, Onion and Mushroom Pâté (p.20).

For an interesting vegetarian main course you could try any of the following:

Pepper Ring Flowers (see p.20)
Aubergine Wedges (see p.92)
Soft Cheese and Vegetable Domes (see p.99)
Parsnip Timbales with Watercress Sauce (see p.82)
Indian Spiced Vegetables (see p.85)
Blue Brie Pancakes (see p.29)
Brioches Stuffed with Mushrooms (see p.22)
Mushroom Risotto (see p.25)
Stir-fried Vegetables with Pasta Bows (see p.80)
Courgettes with Pine Nuts and Lemon Sauce (see p.118)
Tortilla Española (see p.93)
Yellow Peppers with Bulghur (see p.108)
Hot Spiced Onions with Raita (see p.108)
Jacket Potatoes with Creamy Corn Filling (see p.117)
Stuffed Cabbage Leaves with Mushroom Duxelles (see p.109)
Cabbage Rolls with Chestnut Filling (see p.111)

SERVING SUGGESTIONS
Cooking for friends and family should be a pleasure, but sometimes thinking of what to make is almost as hard as finding the time to do it. Here are some ideas:

Nibbles to serve with drinks
Whether you're having a drinks party or wondering what to serve before dinner, you need some alternatives to a bowl of slightly stale crisps or peanuts.

Vegetable Tartlets (see p.28)
Smoked Salmon with Asparagus Tips (see p.25)
Mushroom and Mozzarella Toasts (see p.61)
Aubergine Wedges (see p.92)
Onions Monegasque (see p.92)
Beetroot and Smatana with Crudités (see p.93)
Leek and Corn Rolls (see p.97)
Tortilla Española (see p.93)
Stuffed Vine Leaves (see p.116)
Spinach Parcels with Liver Pâté (see p.116)
Aubergine Dip (see p.35)
Red or Yellow Pepper Coulis with Raw Vegetables (see p.37)
Courgette and Carrot Sticks with Green Mayonnaise (see p.76 and 41)
Crispy Noodles (see p.61)

Spring and summer lunches
Small spring vegetables or ripe summer ones have an incomparably sweet taste. It *is* a trouble to prepare them, but it's worth it for the pleasure they bring after a season of coarser root vegetables or flavourless salads.

Fresh Pea Soup with Mint (see p.50)
Asparagus with Melted Herb Butter (see p.16)
Sugar Peas with Hollandaise Sauce (see p.29)
Navarin of Lamb (see p.68)
Spinach and Fish Terrine (see p.73)
Spring Vegetables with Mint Butter (see p.76)
Vichyssoise of Leek with Watercress (see p.60)
Garden Vegetable Soup (see p.47)
Mange-tout Salad with Avocados and Smoked Turkey (see p.72)

Leeks and Runner Beans with Lemon
Sauce (see p.77)
Summer Vegetable Platter (see p.94)
Tomato and Red Pepper Soup (see p.57)
Globe Artichokes with Vinaigrette Sauce
(see p.17)
Vegetable Kebabs (see p.77)

An autumn buffet supper

In a restricted space you can hardly have a
formal dinner party or even a large stand-
up gathering. Why not invite a dozen
friends to help themselves from a selection
of splendid cold dishes and hot savouries?

Avocado and Broad Bean Salad (see p.27)
Salsify and Courgette Curls (see p.82)
Vegetable Terrine with Mousseline of Fish
(see p.105)
Winter Rice Salad (see p.97)
Taramosalata with Cucumber (see p.21)
Baby Corn, Broccoli and Cheese Salad (see
p.104)
Tossed Salad, with Turbot and French
Beans (see p.96)
Peperonata (see p.18)
Sliced Aubergine Salad (see p.100)
Parsnip and Mushroom Soup (see p.48)
Minestrone Soup with Garlic Toast
Rounds (see p.45 and 61)
Aubergines with Lamb (see p.117)
Hot Spiced Onions with Raita (see p.108)
Peppers with Green Rice and Cheese (see
p.65)
Shallots in Wine with Red Peppers (see
p.104)
Green Cauliflower Salad (see p.101)

Courgette and tomato pasta bake (see p. 73);
Courgette and mushroom ring (see p. 100).

Hot suggestions for cold evenings

Winter food doesn't have to be stodgy but it needs to be appealingly hot. Forget the out-of-season asparagus or salmon and choose steaming soups and stuffed vegetables instead.

Corn and Mushroom Consommé (see p.45)

Courgette and Tomato Pasta Bake (see p.73)

Candied Sweet Potatoes (see p.81)

Parsnip and Mushroom Soup (see p.48)

Crêpes Provençales (see p.72)

Stuffed Cabbage Leaves with Mushroom Duxelles (see p.109)

Aubergines with Cheese (see p.64)

Mushroom and Mozzarella Pancakes (see p.65)

Cream of Tomato Soup (see p.52)

Potato Gratin (see p.84)

Courgette and Almond Soup (see p.48)

Tomatoes with Sole and Two Sauces (see p.71)

Kohlrabi au Gratin (see p.89)

Food for hungry people

If your normal lunch is a couple of biscuits and cheese, it's easy to forget that a hungry student considers a pound of sausages and a plate of chips a 'light snack'. In the long gaps between school or university terms, some of these dishes might provide some filling interludes!

Jacket Potatoes with Creamy Corn Filling (see p.117)

Blue Brie Pancakes with Sliced Avocado and Tomato Sauce (see p.29)

Mushroom Risotto (see p.25)

Potato Ball Soup (see p.49)

Brioches with Creamed Mushrooms (see p.22)

Indian Spiced Vegetables (see p.85)

Spanish Rice with Tomatoes (see p.84)

Sweet Potato Soup with Chestnut Mushrooms (see p.53)

Crispy Top Pasta with Aubergine Sauce (see p.68)

Yellow Peppers with Bulghur (see p.108)

Buttered Corn Cobs (see p.88)

What to do with left-overs?

One of the first lessons in a basic cookery course should be how to deal with the remains of yesterday's beef/potatoes/rice etc. Here are some inventive ways of using them up. Microwaving ensures that they don't look or taste 'reheated'.

Left-over pasta

Stir-fried Vegetables with Pasta Bows (see p.80)

Pasta, Peppers and Peas (see p.101)

Left-over beef, turkey or chicken

Vegetable and Chicken Risotto (see p.64)

Leek and Chicken Soup with Corn (see p.53)

Beef Salad (see p.66)

Left-over potatoes

Salade Niçoise (see p.96)

Chilled Onion Soup (see p.49)

Left-over cooked vegetables

Broccoli and Cauliflower with Cheese Sauce (see p.85)

Spinach with Oil and Garlic (see p.89)

Really fast food

For those who complain that preparing a vegetarian meal takes longer than grilling a chop, here are some suggestions:

Cold Broccoli with Walnut Vinaigrette (see p.16)
Warm Tomatoes with Mozzarella (see p.17)
Mushroom Velvet Soup (see p.55)
Cheese Omelette with Soft Buttered Onions (see p.69)
Stir-fried Beansprouts (see p.88)
Almond, Onion and Mushroom Pâté (see p.20)
Leeks with Red Pepper Rings (see p.24)
Celeriac Soup (see p.56)
Green Salad with Hot Buttered Mushrooms (see p.78)

Slimming with style

The most depressing thing about slimming is the boredom of most diets. Here are some dishes to *enjoy*, to share with those lucky people who aren't on a self-imposed starvation regime, without letting them know that you are:

Celery Soup (see p.52)
Spanish Bean, Asparagus and Egg Salad (see p.24)
Soft Cheese and Vegetable Domes (see p.99)
Gazpacho (see p.57)
Pepper Ring Flowers (see p. 20)
Salmon Trout in Spinach Envelopes (p.71)
Chicken Livers with Chinese Vegetables (see p.69)

Beetroot Borscht with Soured Cream (see p.59)
Courgette and Mushroom Ring (see p.100)
Spinach Quiche Boats (see p.112)
Marrow Stuffed with Minced Beef (see p.113)
Cucumber Trunks with Dill and Fish Salad (see p.113)
Courgettes in Fresh Tomato Sauce (see p.21)
Braised Celery (see p.81)
Cucumber Sauce for Fish (see p.40)

Something surprising

Often the pleasure of eating out is in finding the unexpected – something you hadn't thought of yourself such as an interesting combination or a colourful presentation.

Leek and Cucumber Soup (see p.50)
Courgette and Lamb Moussakas (see p.66)
Parsnip Timbales with Watercress Sauce (see p.82)
Spinach Parcels with Peas (see p.87)
Green Marble Soup (see p.59)
Artichokes with Tomato and Lemon Mousseline (see p.114)
Cabbage Rolls with Chestnut Filling (see p.111)
Sorrel and Pea Soup (see p.56)
Fanned Roast Potatoes (see p.80)
Courgettes with Pine Nuts and Lemon Sauce (see p.118)
Tomatoes and Spaghetti Squash (see p.112)
Pumpkin Soup (see p.61)

INDEX